CW00669964

APM Project
Fundamentals
Qualification (PFQ)

Pull-out Study Guide Planner

APM Project Fundamentals Qualification Study Guide

Association for Project Management

Ibis House, Regent Park

Summerleys Road, Princes Risborough

Buckinghamshire

HP27 9LE

British Library Cataloguing in Publication Data is available.

Paperback ISBN: 978-1-913305-02-4

eISBN: 978-1-913305-03-1

Typeset in 8.5/12pt Poppins by EMC Design Ltd.

Cover design by EMC Design Ltd.

Contents

List of figures and tables

Figures

Tables

Introducing APM

The Association for Project Management (APM) is the only chartered body for the project profession, with over 40,000 individual members and more than 500 organisations participating in our Corporate Partnership Programme.

As a registered educational charity, we are committed to developing and promoting the value of project management in order to deliver improved project outcomes for the benefit of society.

There are a number of ways in which you can benefit from what we do, including:

* membership
* qualifications
* chartered status
* publications
* events

Inspiring positive change – our vision and mission

Our vision for the profession is ambitious, challenging and radical. Above all, it reflects what society expects: a world in which all projects succeed.

Our mission is: to advance the science, theory and practice of project and programme management for the public benefit.

Our strategic themes

The environment for project delivery is complex. The project profession needs strong, consistent leadership to build the profile it warrants, challenge the status quo where it matters and set the highest standards.

Our mission and charitable objects are underpinned by four strategic themes that provide us with clear direction.

1 APM provides leadership of the profession
2 APM is a professional body for all project professionals
3 APM identifies and enables the right skills for the project professional
4 APM is an outstanding professional body

About the author

Raymond Stadnik has over 30 years' experience of delivering change within a wide range of organisations throughout the world. Part of that time he has focused on developing the competence of people, through either classroom-based training or more intensive coaching events.

Raymond has now brought that experience to bear on the production of the *APM Project Fundamentals Qualification Study Guide*. The guide attempts to follow the APM project life cycle format as closely as possible, suggesting a study timeline that mirrors a project timeline.

> *"A timeline is a very important feature of any project. The study guide should be written taking timing into account. Sections of the guide should start with organisational context, strategy, concept, planning, execution, handover and closure, then benefits and outcomes. There are two choices here for the learner: study project management academically topic by topic, or as an unfolding project, building as it progresses. The latter option may also be more in line with any project management experience a user may have already observed. From a teaching perspective, candidates who have studied project management using a timed sequence that mirrors an actual project's sequence achieve greater exam success."*

Raymond Stadnik FAPM, author.

Chapter 1

Study planning

1.1 Using this guide

This study guide has one main objective: to support you in your study for the APM Project Fundamentals Qualification (PFQ). It is also hoped that this guide will act as a reference after your success has been rewarded and that it will occupy a deserved place on your bookshelf, helping you to solve your real-life project management dilemmas for years to come.

If you are using this guide as a means of self-study, it is expected that about 25–30 hours would be a good average time to devote to becoming exam ready. This time includes planning, reading and attempting the quick quizzes and some sample questions found in Chapter 3.

When using this guide, think about your approach to learning in three layers. The first layer is the main subject text: this is knowledge that relates directly to the learning outcomes and assessment criteria. This layer is the sufficient amount of study required to be prepared to sit the PFQ exam. To further support your learning, you may consider how project management influences your work and day-to-day activity. This is where a second layer of learning may be useful. Each subject has a 'Think about . . .' opportunity where learners can consider projects that they may have some experience of, or where their organisation is carrying out activity that requires a project management approach.

Sometimes during the learning of any subject, it can be difficult to imagine just how some of the theory, techniques and processes can actually be used in real-life practice, particularly if you are new to project management. That's where the third and final layer of learning can provide some valuable insight into just how real projects deliver what is required, actually using the very elements that you are about to study. The features on 'The world of project management', which accompany some of the subject areas, provide examples of just how projects are managed in the real world using examples drawn from recent editions of APM's quarterly journal, *Project*.

So, even with no practical project management experience, this guide and the associated APM materials will help get you started as you prepare for the PFQ exam. Provided, of course, you apply sufficient personal effort to execute your plan.

When you first view this guide, the syllabus, candidate guidance and other available material you are planning to use, you might think that there are a lot of different numbering systems that may not seem to be connected. Well, you are not alone. That's probably a common first challenge experienced by most people wanting to tackle a substantial subject like project management. It is, however, essential that you do get to grips with the complete structure very early on and incorporate this into your study planning. These introductory pages will help bring all the different components together.

PFQ learning structure

The most important document for an initial review is the APM Project Fundamentals Qualification Syllabus: learning outcomes and assessment criteria aligned to the *APM Body of Knowledge 7th edition*. You can download the syllabus from the APM website. The syllabus highlights the 10 learning outcomes that describe the knowledge you are required to demonstrate at a sufficient level to be awarded the PFQ qualification. The learning outcomes contain 59 assessment criteria, which aim to show you what specific knowledge is being examined for each learning outcome. Ultimately your knowledge will be tested through 60 individual multiple-choice exam questions.

The content of this learning guide will help you to accumulate the necessary insight to demonstrate your knowledge to the required level for this qualification. There are 15 study areas contained in the study guide. Each study area fulfils the knowledge requirements for one or more assessment criteria. The relationship between the study guide, assessment criteria and learning outcomes is shown in Figure 1.1.1.

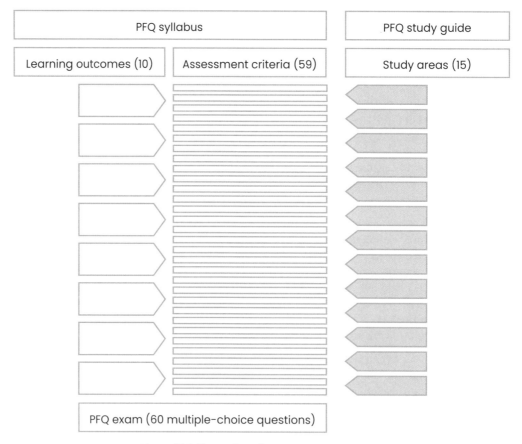

Figure 1.1.1 Illustration of PFQ learning structure

Study guide planner

To help you plan your study and monitor your progress, you can use the PFQ study guide planner. It shows the 15 study areas grouped into the three main sections of the guide and mapped directly to each learning outcome. As you complete the study of a particular subject, you can then tick it off on the planner, keeping track of your progress. You will find that the study areas are overlaid onto the project life cycle, showing how the subjects relate to the sequence of a project. This provides a rough outline of how a project might develop, which may be helpful if you do not yet have any practical project management experience. In reality a lot of the subject areas discuss processes and frameworks that probably happen simultaneously and throughout the whole life cycle, rather than starting and stopping as the study guide suggests. See the study guide planner as more of a revision aid rather than an example of an actual project plan.

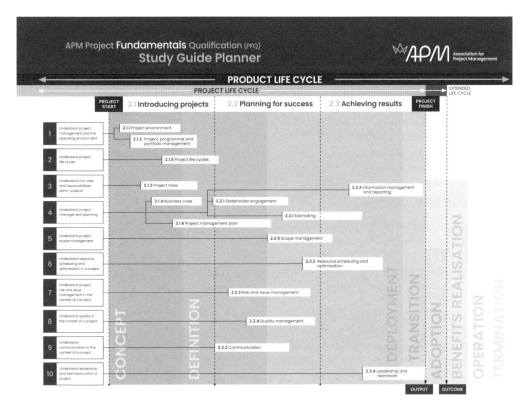

Figure 1.1.2 Pull-out study guide planner

Other supporting documentation

In addition to the syllabus, you are advised to download the *APM Project Fundamentals Qualification Guide for Candidates*. This will provide you with information concerning the exam procedures, exam marking and notifications.

You should also download the latest version of the PFQ exam sample paper. This contains examples of questions of a similar style to those found in the live exam. This paper will give you a feel for the actual exam and build your familiarity with the paper prior to your exam day.

Visit the PFQ information section of the qualifications page of the APM website. Information is regularly updated and published to help and support candidates taking the exam.

APM Body of Knowledge 7th edition

This study guide and the supporting documentation will assist you in studying for and sitting the PFQ exam. You may also consider purchasing the *APM Body of Knowledge*. While this is not strictly necessary for PFQ study, as a lot of the content of this study guide is taken directly from the *APM Body of Knowledge*, you might find some of its other topics and content of interest in the future.

1.2 How to study

You will have your own preferences and approach to the way you learn, and they will influence the way you use this material. Many candidates find that self-study is just as effective as classroom-based courses, while for others the discipline and self-motivation required for going it alone is just too demanding.

There are many benefits, therefore, in deciding early on how you are going to schedule your studies in relation to all the other activities in your daily life. By thinking about these aspects now, you are likely to benefit from a more enjoyable and meaningful learning experience. This in turn will improve overall effectiveness and enable you to adopt a more flexible approach to answering questions.

Suggested approaches

Consider the relationship between practice and theory, investigate typical projects in your working environment, or do some online research into projects that you hear about on your local news or in the press. This type of research will allow you to appreciate the connection between the theory and common practice out there in the real world.

After completing each subject, look for opportunities where you can apply some of the tools and techniques that you are learning. In addition to theoretical study, application and appropriate feedback are essential for effective learning. There are likely to be opportunities to apply theory in your workplace, in social activities and in the home, for example, a work-based project, a club project or a DIY project.

You may be able to review past projects and discuss project management performance with experienced project managers within your organisation, or friends and family members who may work in a project environment. You can obtain feedback on your own study performance from peers, colleagues and supervisors, and there may be opportunities to form study groups or social networks with others who are also studying for the PFQ.

All of the activities discussed above can enhance your learning experience significantly. However, you will need to be proactive in identifying opportunities and include them in your learning plan. Remember that a plan means nothing until it is executed; ensure you take action.

Setting personal learning objectives and realistic targets

On average, the core study time required is about 25–30 hours, including reading, doing quizzes and answering sample questions. Additional time will be required for any optional learning activities, extra revision sessions, attendance at coaching workshops and final exam preparation.

The targeted time frame for study is only a suggestion and may vary considerably depending on personal time constraints and any previous experience of the subject matter. It is, therefore, important to establish the feasibility of the target date you have set for taking the exam and allow adequate study time. The key here is to be realistic. If you dive into study to get to the exam as soon as possible, your approach may not take into account all the other activities that, up to this point, have gone by unnoticed and are now also making demands on your time. This is when you start missing your goals and become disheartened, and the plan is now in shreds. The opposite can be just as challenging, where you purchase the guide, don't bother with a plan but start reading from page 1 expecting to complete the guide at some point in the future. Months go by and guess what? You still haven't got past page 10 and you have read page 8 about 50 times!

What is needed, of course, is a balanced approach that allows you to study, work and carry on your social and family life as normally as possible. Tell your friends, family and work colleagues what you are doing and the commitment you are expecting to make to gain a very worthwhile qualification. They will be glad to support you and, of course, join in the celebrations when you get a great pass in the exam.

Common learning techniques

Mind mapping

A mind map is a powerful graphic technique that provides a universal key to unlock the potential of the brain. It harnesses the full range of cortical skills – word, image, number, logic, rhythm, colour and spatial awareness – in a single, uniquely powerful manner. In so doing, it gives you the freedom to roam the infinite expanses of your brain. A mind map can be applied to every aspect of life where improved learning and clearer thinking will enhance human performance.

Widely used in learning, mind maps were first developed in the late 1960s by Tony Buzan. Mind maps are now used by millions of people around the world – from the very young to the very old – whenever they wish to learn or use their minds more effectively. Mind maps can be applied to most of life's situations that involve any learning or thinking.

If it has been some time since you last studied, you might find mind maps helpful. An online search for 'mind maps' will give you more information.

Prompt lists and checklists

If you are new to project management, the number of terms and sheer volume of material may seem a little overwhelming. Breaking down larger concepts into lists can often be a good way of taking control of the material. Starting with each of the larger subject areas, a hierarchy of related terms can be developed, and then these can be broken down into other associated terms.

Lists of terms can be useful, and lists of questions or prompts can also aid learning. Ideal if you have a daily commute, using lists is an easy way to revise and can be a break from reading and then re-reading the material.

Flash cards

'A picture paints a thousand words' is a commonly quoted saying to describe the effect of using visual imagery as a substitute for lengthy text-based information. When these images are created by learners and placed on small cards, they can act as aides-memoires to revise and learn fundamental concepts. Learners report increased success rates in exams when flash cards are used.

Flash cards can be used to show images or very short text descriptions, and can be created by hand or on a computer and then printed for use. There are also a number of free software applications that allow the development of digital flash cards that can be reviewed on a phone, tablet or laptop. An online search for 'flash cards' will provide some insight into this potentially powerful learning aid.

Study groups

If you work for an organisation where project management is a common practice, the chances are that there will be others learning project management at the same time as you. Ask those around you whether they know of anyone and discuss your course generally with your colleagues. They may be interested in what you are doing, so much so they may also decide to study for a project management qualification.

Preparing and studying with others may mean that you can share ideas, test each other and discuss some of the more practical applications of project management within your organisation. It is often satisfying to share areas of learning that you find more difficult with others who may also find the same areas challenging. Together you are able to piece together the solution and gain the satisfaction of solving what was seen as a learning obstacle.

Chapter 2

Study areas

2.1 Introducing projects

Organisations operate in a dynamic context, full of uncertainty, novelty and turbulence. This section identifies just how organisations can use projects, programmes and portfolios in order to enhance performance, bring about change and enable organisations to adapt, improve and grow. Project work therefore represents intentional investment in development, enhancement and improvement.

The need for investment emerges from the aspirational plans and an overarching purpose that transpire from the strategic intent of an organisation. Project work encompasses strategic investments that enable assets, structures, systems, activities and capabilities to be formed, maintained or enhanced so that the organisational plans and ambitions can be realised.

Organisational change is introduced through projects, programmes and portfolios in order to deliver business value. The business value is accrued through the realisation of benefits that result from project work. Benefits are part of ensuring that investments are made to deliver value to the organisation. This normally applies even when the project is being done by a supplier or contracting organisation, or if the work is needed to maintain current capability, or in order to conform to new regulations or directives so that smooth business operations can be allowed to proceed.

The successful deployment of change, the support of new behaviours and the utilisation of new capability, resulting in the realisation of benefits, involves engaging with, promoting and working with diverse communities and groups. To ensure that value is created and sustained, organisations need to consider and address the full investment life cycle, ensuring that forecast benefits materialise.

Delivering strategy is enabled through the use of projects, programmes and portfolios. Portfolios structure investments in line with strategic objectives, while balancing, aligning and scrutinising capacity and resources. Programmes combine business-as-usual (steady-state) activities with projects dictated by strategic priorities. Projects are transient endeavours that bring about change and achieve planned objectives. Together, they combine to deliver the beneficial change required to implement, enable and satisfy the strategic intent of the organisation.

This section is the start of the learning journey and includes:

2.1.1 **Project environment**

2.1.2 **Project, programme and portfolio management**

2.1.3 **Project roles**

2.1.4 **Business case**

2.1.5 **Project life cycles**

2.1.6 **Project management plan**

2.1.1 Project environment

Learning objectives

This section introduces one of the main reasons why projects exist in the first place. The environment is defined as the societal and/or organisational setting of a project, programme or portfolio, also described as the project context. By examining the project context, stakeholders will understand how the project being considered relates to the environment.

By the time you have studied this section you will have completed the following:

Learning outcome	Assessment criteria
1 Understand project management and the operating environment	1.6 Describe why PESTLE analysis might be used by a project manager

Every organisation is faced with a constantly changing environment that creates problems, opportunities or business needs that require some degree of response if threats are to be minimised, opportunities exploited and business needs effectively addressed. Every project is a response to the changing environment. Within that environment are the factors that influence and impact projects, as shown in Figure 2.1.1.1.

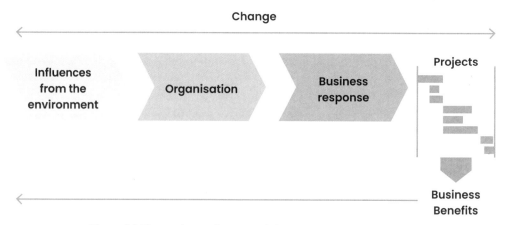

Figure 2.1.1.1 How the environment influences an organisation

Organisations must develop a strategic approach to managing change. Projects deliver the beneficial change required to implement, enable and satisfy the strategic intent of the organisation. Practically this will be achieved by deploying new assets, functions, capabilities, processes, structures and systems.

Why PESTLE analysis might be used by a project manager

The environment is the driving force for the project. It is important for the project manager to understand how these drivers are likely to influence the project. They may impact how the project manager delivers the project, what they deliver, who is involved and when it needs to be delivered. Early on in the project the answers to some of these questions may be uncertain. As a result, planning needs to be flexible, options need to be effectively evaluated and various scenarios assessed in order for the project to emerge as the optimum solution to what might be a range of diverse needs.

The impact of infrastructure, physical environment, mitigating the potential adverse impacts of other projects and the project's technology are just some of the factors the project manager must take into account when planning the delivery of a project. Short-term practical implementation impacts of the project, as well as its conceptual development and consequent long-term impacts, also need to be fully considered. In addition, project managers need to be attuned to internal aspects such as the cultural, organisational and social environments of the project's sponsoring organisation.

Understanding this environment includes identifying the project's stakeholders and their ability to affect its successful outcome. This means working with people to achieve the best results, especially if the project is based in a highly technical or complex environment. Therefore, it is essential that the project manager and the project team are comfortable with, and sympathetic towards, their physical, technological, cultural, organisational and social surroundings. The objective is the influencing of the project environment in a positive way or changing the way the project is being delivered, all with the aim of gaining a better reception for the change that the project is designed to introduce.

Resistance to change may be evident among some of the stakeholders, while others may have vested interests, or personal or group agendas that are only indirectly related to the project. It is important that these interests are identified and categorised proactively and in a timely manner so that the corresponding risks, which may otherwise undermine the success of the project, can be significantly reduced. Failure to take such an approach could lead to a less than optimum project outcome.

Every project team member needs to develop the attitude that, just as they are stakeholders, every other project stakeholder is also important. There should be a commitment to service and the creation of a project management environment in which every decision and action is designed to make the stakeholder's experience better than it would have been had the project not been implemented. It requires a focus on the quality of the stakeholders' experience at every stage of the project.

There are a number of common forms of environmental analysis, from simple external/ internal factor analysis to ones using a more specific framework. One of the more common forms of analysis for the project environment is PESTLE analysis, a management technique to help project management understand the environment in which the project operates.

PESTLE analysis is a popular method of examining the many different factors affecting an organisation and a project – the external or internal influences on success or failure. The impact of these factors on the project may be differentiated in six ways:

- **Political** – Current and potential influences from political pressures.
- **Economic** – Local, national and world economic impact.
- **Sociological** – The effect of changes in the needs of society.
- **Technological** – New and emerging technology.
- **Legal** – Local, national and world legislation.
- **Environmental** – Local, national and world environmental issues.

These six factors may be considered across the whole of the organisation, or within specific business areas or in a specific project, and could be considered to be external only, internal only or both, in order to determine the likely effects. Business areas could include:

- customers/technology
- industry/marketplace/intermediaries
- competitors/stakeholders
- supply sources/time
- internal capability/governance requirements

Following PESTLE analysis, an organisation would most likely have a number of options available as to how the desired objectives could be achieved. One strength of a business case for a project is that a number of options have been considered and that there is evidence to show that the organisation has not become over-reliant on a single idea, when there may be other more favourable options available.

Think about...

an organisation you are familiar with and write down some of the aspects of its environment that would influence projects being considered by that organisation. Use the PESTLE framework to help.

Read about... The world of project management

The subject that you have just studied shows how the project needs to be responsive to the driving forces of the environment and particularly the areas that are important to stakeholders. Traditionally, project managers have had to balance the common areas of the environment with the commercial aspects of delivering the project, namely the cost of delivery, the time taken and the performance of the output of the project within the operations of the business requiring the change to take place.

More recent approaches suggest that project management should also consider sustainability in addition to managing social, environmental and economic aspects of the environment. This relatively new consideration is demanding a greater degree of engagement with stakeholders to create projects that will ultimately lead to more sustainable development of an organisation or society.

A project delivered by engineering, design and consultancy company Ramboll for the British Antarctic Survey (BAS) shows how sustainability can be balanced alongside traditional environmental considerations and still derive technical capability from what is actually delivered.

Frame, plan, adapt, measure

Ramboll's Bruce Wulff is working with BAS to upgrade its facilities. Given that BAS is a research-driven organisation and is committed to environmental stewardship, sustainability is a key priority.

"There are more than 60 separate task orders within the programme, so, to ensure a consistent approach to sustainability, a programme-wide steering group was established," Wulff says. "It includes the client and all stakeholder groups, and sets an overall strategy. It means we can build a sustainability management plan [SMP] for each project, based on the relevant parts of the UN's Sustainable Development Goals."

Some project measures are obvious: upgraded buildings are designed around careful analysis of usage patterns and suitability of on-site renewable energy technology, for example. But, even in the Antarctic, looking at local sourcing is a key sustainability win.

"We are building a new wharf capable of berthing the new, larger research vessel, the *Sir David Attenborough*," says Wulff. "We needed massive rock-fill, but rather than ship it in, we opened up a small borrow-pit nearby. That not only slashed the carbon footprint for transport, it also minimised the risk of introducing invasive species."

But Wulff stresses this in-the-field sustainability decision-making is empowered by a clear SMP, which must be bedded in from the start. It helps, he adds, to have a collegiate client in BAS, which endorsed a partnership approach right through each project's supply chain.

That's typified by the programme's sustainability metrics, some of which are captured in key performance indicators (KPIs) for each project. At quarterly updates with the client and construction partners, these form a key part of the discussion.

Originally published in *Project* Winter 2019.

If you would like to read more about this example or other real-world project examples, copies of APM's *Project* journal can be downloaded from the members' resources area of the APM website: apm.org.uk/project.

2.1.2 Project, programme and portfolio management

Learning objectives

This section introduces the three layers of management involved in delivering change to the organisation. The overall strategy is set through the use of portfolio management and that strategy is delivered using programme management to ensure benefits are realised. None of this could be achieved without the delivery of each individual project using project management.

By the time you have studied this section you will have completed the following:

Learning outcome	Assessment criteria
1 Understand project management and the operating environment	1.1 Define the term 'project'
	1.2 State the differences between a project and business-as-usual
	1.3 Define the term 'project management'
	1.4 State the key purpose of project management
	1.5 Define the terms 'programme management' and 'portfolio management' and their relationship with project management

The term 'project'

Projects are unique, transient endeavours, undertaken to bring about change and achieve planned objectives. A project is usually deemed to be a success if it achieves the objectives according to its acceptance criteria, normally within an agreed timescale and budget. Project work is conducted across normal organisational functional areas, setting up a temporary organisation, drawing on the skills, expertise and knowledge of the organisation, as well as third parties where appropriate.

Projects normally use capital expenditure to acquire, upgrade and maintain assets, services, products and capability. Projects need to take into account the ultimate requirements for decommissioning and disposal.

In some settings, it is possible to find arrangements involving multiple projects running in parallel, or related to one another, to provide support or to build additional capabilities. Multiple concurrent projects may require prioritisation in terms of scheduled deployment, importance of primary deliverables or the availability of key resources, skills or individuals.

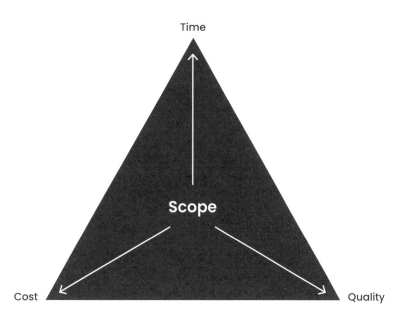

Figure 2.1.2.1 Triple constraints of time, cost and quality

The project delivery environment is always considered to be constrained. That is, to obtain the value required from delivering the project it has to be delivered within a certain time and for the required budget, and it must deliver the specification, quality and performance characteristics that will be sufficient for those who are going to use the output of the project to gain the benefits required. The value of these benefits must be greater than the investment required to deliver the project's output. All projects trade the triple constraints of time, cost and quality to achieve the defined scope of the project as shown in Figure 2.1.2.1.

Differences between a project and business-as-usual

The term 'business-as-usual', (BAU) refers to an organisation's normal day-to-day operations. It can also be referred to as steady-state. Projects contrast with BAU in a number of ways. It is important for the success of the project that the project's unique characteristics are recognised and that the most appropriate structures, management and controls are put in place.

Five common characteristics of projects and how they differ from BAU are shown in Table 2.1.2.1.

Feature	Projects	Business-as-usual
Purpose	Achieve objectives then terminate	Sustain the organisation to achieve its business purpose and goals
Timescale	Limited, temporary in nature, predefined start and end points	Ongoing, no defined end point
Outcome	Unique product or service	Repetitive, non-unique product, service or result
People	Temporary teams, formed across organisational boundaries to meet project needs. May not be aligned with organisational structure	Teams formed within organisational structure and aligned to suit functional demands
Management	Dedicated manager appointed for the duration of project only; may not have direct line authority over project team	Long-term formal management, direct line authority over functional unit personnel

Table 2.1.2.1 Differences between projects and BAU

Typically, a project's objective is to deliver outputs, for example, a software solution, a building, a process or a service. The project team transitions the outputs to an internal or external client to deliver the desired outcomes and benefits. Sometimes, the project also includes the work required to deliver outcomes and benefits. In such cases, the project team leads more of the work to deliver the changes required by the client to realise the project's intended benefits.

BAU, on the other hand, uses the products of the project to realise the benefits. It is unusual for projects to deliver any benefits into the organisation during their deployment (unless there is some form of phased roll-out, or a delivery contractor benefits by being paid to deliver specific phases).

The term 'project management'

Project management is the application of processes, methods, skills, knowledge and experience to achieve specific project objectives for change according to the project acceptance criteria within agreed parameters. Project management has finite deliverables that are constrained to a finite timescale and budget.

A key factor that distinguishes project management from just 'management' is that it has this final deliverable and a constrained timespan, unlike management, which is an ongoing process. Because of this a project manager needs a wide range of skills: often technical skills, and certainly people management skills and good business awareness.

Project managers must understand the relative priorities of time, cost and quality as important parts of the decision as to which management approach will suit best.

The key purpose of project management

Change poses difficulties for organisations because of the complex relationships between the business environment, the organisation, its people and supporting technologies; any change in one aspect will affect one or more of the others. A structured approach to change is more likely to mean that the change is successful and the business gains only a positive effect from the change. Approaching change in this structured way is the foundation of project management. Think of change as a project and the best way to manage change is to use project management.

Projects bring about change and enable organisations to adapt, improve and grow. Project work therefore represents intentional investment in development, enhancement and improvement.

The terms 'programme management' and 'portfolio management' and their relationship with project management

Programmes can be defined as unique, transient, strategic endeavours undertaken to achieve beneficial change, and they incorporate a group of related projects and business-as-usual (steady-state) activities. The distinction between projects and programmes depends on the context and the guiding criteria between them often relates to the complexity of scope and the addition of change activities. The need for significant improvement will be consistent with the organisation's strategy, and programmes will help to deliver elements of that strategy.

Programmes typically combine new deployment with some elements of business-as-usual. Consequently, they use capital expenditure to acquire assets, services, products and capability, alongside meeting operating expenses incurred as a result of performing normal business operations.

Programmes are often defined as delivering change, and would typically incorporate the full utilisation of benefits to satisfy the business case. The overall measure of success is determined by the actual realisation of the expected benefits, which frequently involves the use of capabilities or facilities created by the programme in an ongoing, business-as-usual manner.

Portfolios are used to select, prioritise and control an organisation's programmes and projects, in line with its strategic objectives and capacity to deliver. Their goal is to balance the implementation of change initiatives and the maintenance of business-as-usual, while optimising return on investment. It would be typical for organisations to have projects that were part of a programme, part of a portfolio or stand-alone. The latter would be where the project would be managed independently by the host organisation of any existing programme or portfolio as shown in Figure 2.1.2.2.

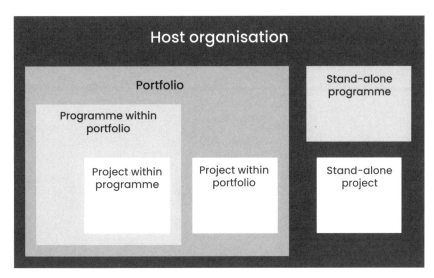

Figure 2.1.2.2 Projects, programmes and portfolios situated to deliver strategic change

Portfolios are used to structure investments. They can be managed at an organisational or functional level (e.g. including all IT initiatives) to optimise strategic benefits or operational efficiency, respectively. They address a number of major questions:

- Are these the projects and programmes needed to deliver the strategic objectives, subject to risk, resource constraints and affordability?
- Is the organisation delivering them effectively and efficiently?
- Are the full potential benefits from the organisation's investment being realised?

Portfolios are particularly concerned with the interdependencies between projects and programmes in terms of:

- scarce or limited resources
- balance within the portfolio (e.g. between risks and returns)
- alignment with the strategic intent and main priorities
- timing
- capacity bottlenecks (where a number of projects need access to a scarce resource at the same time)

Portfolio success relates to the soundness of the investment and depends on the ability to address the above concerns and questions. The management of a structured portfolio involves constant review of the balance of investment and benefit, creating and closing projects and programmes as required.

Think about...

an organisation you are familiar with and write down five features of business-as-usual and five different features of projects.

Read about... The world of project management

Some of the largest organisations in the world use portfolio management to enable their businesses to succeed in a rapidly changing environment. A prime example of this was an article written for APM's *Project* journal by John McIntyre where he explained how Silicon Valley's Objectives and Key Results approach to strategy and portfolio management will allow projects to flex and adapt.

This excerpt from John's article shows how Google tackles portfolio management.

From start-up Google to portfolio management

When Google was a start-up, it used the Objectives and Key Results (OKRs) framework to define where it was going, to align its teams and to set itself ambitious targets. The framework has scaled with it and is still in use today. OKRs are defined at the highest level and are cascaded down. Everyone understands the vision, which is encapsulated by the objectives and measured by the associated key results. Individuals are granted the flexibility to set their own OKRs too, so that the top-down objectives are balanced with bottom-up objectives, which serve to prevent a silo mentality building up.

How does this link to portfolio management? As someone with a projects background, my approach to portfolio management mirrored my approach to projects. Lock down the scope and plan, then manage risk. The portfolio plan was usually constructed as a sum of the projects that were running within it. The portfolio outcomes were derived from the benefits we expected to see from the projects. If the outcomes broadly aligned with the business plan, then all was good. We had a portfolio plan! If not, we would make changes, swapping projects out and adding initiatives in – balancing capacity with requirement until we felt that we had it right.

Originally published in *Project* Winter 2019.

If you would like to read more about this example or other real-world project examples, copies of APM's *Project* journal can be downloaded from the members' resources area of the APM website: apm.org.uk/project.

2.1.3 Project roles

Learning objectives

This section introduces the key roles that are members of a typical project organisation structure. Projects are temporary endeavours and therefore, by definition, have a temporary structure established by the people in the permanent organisation to manage activities and resources to deliver specific objectives within predetermined time frames.

By the time you have studied this section you will have completed the following:

Learning outcome	Assessment criteria
3 Understand the roles and responsibilities within projects	**3.1** Outline project management roles and responsibilities (including the project sponsor, project manager, project governance, project team members, end users, product owner and the project management office)

One of the biggest challenges faced by the project manager in creating the project organisation is defining the roles that are necessary. The project has a different culture to the day-to-day organisation. Most of the roles are cross-functional team activities, where the traditional organisational hierarchy dissolves. Distinct roles need to be clearly defined and the relationship between them fully established; this not only promotes teamwork but also ensures a complete coverage of responsibilities and ownership. A typical project organisation structure is shown in Figure 2.1.3.1.

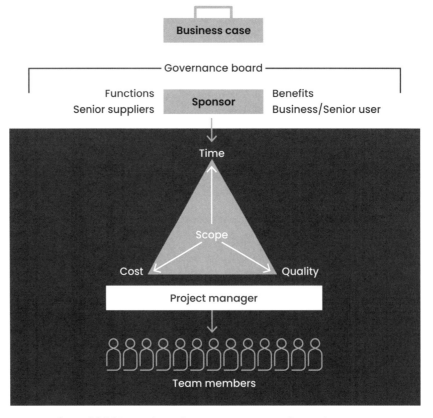

Figure 2.1.3.1 Example project management roles and structure

The roles and responsibilities of the project sponsor

The sponsor is the individual considered the primary risk taker and has ultimate accountability and overall responsibility for the project. The sponsor will most likely have managed the project through the initial phase. Once the business case has been approved a project manager will be appointed to take over delivery of the project. The sponsor remains accountable for ensuring that the project's benefits are realised when the project is handed over to operations.

The sponsor is a member of and has the delegated authority of the steering group, as a chairperson, to assist with business management and project management issues that arise outside the formal duties of the steering group. The sponsor also lends support by advocacy at a senior level and ensures that the necessary resources (both financial and human) are available to the project. The project champion, corporate client and project sponsor may be the same person for some projects.

Sponsor responsibilities include:

- being the arbiter for user and stakeholder requirements through chairing of the steering group
- determining the relative priority of time, cost and quality
- initiating the project and ensuring a project manager is appointed
- monitoring high-level project progress and making control decisions when necessary and when escalated by the project manager
- monitoring the project's business environment and reviewing the business case at gate reviews
- keeping senior management informed of project progress
- terminating the project if necessary, after gate review
- providing ongoing support to the project manager
- developing and maintaining ownership of the business case

The roles and responsibilities of the project manager

The project manager's role is to plan, organise, staff, motivate, evaluate, direct, control and lead the project from start to finish and to deliver the project objectives.

Project manager responsibilities include:

- delivering the project to time, cost and quality/performance priorities
- making timely decisions to ensure project success
- communicating with the sponsor, informing them of progress and seeking direction when necessary to aid success
- managing sponsor and user expectations
- defining and planning the project through the creation of the project management plan
- monitoring and controlling project progress
- building, leading and motivating the project team throughout the project
- ensuring work packages are allocated and the responsibilities identified
- keeping the sponsor and senior management informed of progress/problems/issues
- initiating reviews and assisting the sponsor in making the decision to terminate the project, if justified
- communicating and acting as prime point of contact with team members, other organisations, contractors, suppliers and operations representatives

The roles and responsibilities of project governance

Governance in the project is implemented through a governance board that comprises representatives of the functions and departments within the organisation who are investing in, or being impacted by, the project, programme or portfolio.

The members of the governance board have responsibility for overseeing deployment and making decisions throughout the chosen life cycle in a way that is commensurate with the size and complexity of the work being undertaken. Governance boards have a variety of titles, including steering committee, steering group, project board, programme boards, etc. The extent and limit of a governance board's authority is defined by terms of reference or a board charter, typically developed by the sponsor. This board will influence each project in a number of ways, for example:

- Projects will have a relevant business case to secure funding and assess initial and ongoing feasibility.
- All projects will follow a recognised project life cycle, used to transfer governance to each project through phases with various control points, such as gate reviews, audits and evaluation reviews.
- The organisation will seek to agree a structured methodology for the delivery of projects ensuring that there is consistency of practice throughout the whole organisation.
- Clearly defined processes and documentation maintained throughout the delivery of the project, such as the project management plan, will ensure that all project management activities are to best-practice principles.
- More effective decision-making is carried out at stage gates where the sponsor can initiate a review of the project, taking account of the current environment and impact of change.
- Reporting and escalation routes with clearly defined roles and responsibilities will ensure prompt attention to and control of risk and issues.
- Effective quality management will ensure the effective use of quality assurance and independent audit processes.

The roles and responsibilities of project team members

Project team members may stay with the project throughout its life or may only join the team to carry out a specific task. The primary role of the project team is to support the project manager in managing the project to meet its objectives, by providing the combined expertise to allow the project objectives and scope to be correctly identified and achieved.

Specific responsibilities may include:

- managing communication with stakeholders as assigned in the communication plan
- managing sections of the work breakdown structure (identifying tasks, estimating, monitoring, problem-solving, ensuring completion to the specified quality, on time and within budget)
- acting as risk owner and effectively managing risk within their area of expertise
- supporting the project manager and other team members in solving project-wide problems (acting as action owners)
- contributing to the evaluation of the project at all stages and reviews

The roles and responsibilities of end users

Users are accountable for specifying operational requirements and for accepting and operating the deliverables to achieve the defined benefits.

User responsibilities include:

- identifying project requirements, ensuring objective separation of 'must-haves' and 'wants'
- identifying project constraints and dependencies
- accepting and operating the deliverables
- providing practical assistance and guidance through a user representative or senior user as part of the steering group structure if it exists
- assisting the project manager with handover/acceptance
- informing the project manager of any operational changes that may influence delivery
- actively participating as a member of the project team

The roles and responsibilities of the product owner

The product owner's main contribution is to lead the focus on product development. Very much part of an agile approach, they have strong expertise and deep knowledge of stakeholders' needs and can act as the intermediary between stakeholders and those team members delivering the project.

Product owner responsibilities include:

- defining goals and creating vision for the operability of the project's outputs
- communicating with stakeholders to ensure that the project remains aligned with business objectives
- providing feedback to the project team on task dependencies, constraints, priorities and progress in relation to business needs
- establishing priorities for scope, budget and time with relation to stakeholder requirements
- acting as the primary communication link between stakeholders and teams, ensuring stakeholder buy-in, linking major decisions with strategy and providing clear instructions and outlines of deliverables to product developers
- evaluating progress, providing feedback to the team on delivery performance and advising if continuation is feasible

The roles and responsibilities of the project management office (PMO)

When an organisation is responsible for delivering many simultaneous projects there will be management tasks that are common to all of these projects. Other common areas could include information management, governance services, reporting and general administration. It could benefit an organisation if these common needs could be brought together to form a central core of services to all projects the organisation delivers. This could be achieved through the creation of a PMO.

The payback gained by any organisation undertaking considerable investment in a PMO could be improved deployment support, process improvement and increased resource flexibility. In addition, PMOs can provide access to services that might never be justified for a single project, for example:

- **Controls and reporting** – Collecting, analysing and presenting progress information and managing interdependencies.
- **Assurance** – Audits, health checks and reviews to support decision gates and change control.
- **Centre of excellence** – Improving processes, tools and techniques; embedding best practice through training and support; and measuring capabilities to review progress and target higher levels of maturity.
- **Specialist support** – Provision of specialist skills such as risk, quality, planning or finance resources as role models to other project professionals.
- **Information management** – Document management and access to information, tools and services.

Think about...

a project you are familiar with and write down who would fill the following roles:

Role	Individual
Sponsor	
Project manager	
End user	
Product owner	

If you can't think of projects you are familiar with, try some online research. Search 'UK projects' and consider some of the options shown.

2.1.4 Business case

Learning objectives

This section considers the business case, which provides the justification for undertaking a project or programme. It evaluates the benefit, cost and risk of alternative options and provides a rationale for the preferred solution. The very first consideration of a project by the organisation provides the opportunity to evaluate the options that may be available.

By the time you have studied this section you will have completed the following:

Learning outcome	Assessment criteria
4. Understand project management planning	**4.4** Outline the purpose and typical content of a business case
	4.5 Explain the role of a project sponsor and project manager in relation to developing a business case
	4.7 Define the term 'benefits management'

Purpose and typical content of a business case

All organisations, either private or public, must be accountable for how funds are used and the level of returns gained from these funding decisions. The business case provides a recognised framework through which project spending proposals can be recorded, reviewed and audited to learn lessons about how efficiently the organisation is deploying funds to achieve its targeted returns.

The business case will be referred to throughout the project in order to make decisions about the continuing viability of supporting the change initiative. Reviews will be carried out at the end of and prior to starting major project phases, with the intention of avoiding continued investment when it appears unlikely that the project will achieve the returns that justify such funding. A decision to terminate a project could be for a number of reasons. A changing economic environment may cause increases in the cost of providing funding, and therefore increase costs to an unacceptable level. The output being delivered may be forecast to not deliver the benefits that were planned. Societal trends may mean that the output is no longer a desirable commodity for the intended user population.

Typical business case content

At the highest level the business case will show the level of investment required, the change intended and the resulting benefits. An environmental analysis may show the distinct background and business drivers stimulating the organisation at this time. The detail of how this is documented can vary depending on the business sector of the sponsoring organisation and the level of accountability expected. There are, however, some fundamental aspects that would be common to most business situations.

Background/situation – This will capture the essence of why the project is needed, including information such as environmental analysis, market situation and the output of any research studies that have been carried out. The information in this section should clearly state the problem, opportunity or business need the project is intended to address.

Benefits – A full agreement on how the benefits will be realised and measured, and how the stakeholders will be involved, is crucial to ultimate feasibility. This information should be sufficient for stakeholders to understand the operations and ongoing maintenance required to enable the acceptance and use of the benefits.

Budget – This refers to the funds that are expected to be consumed as a result of delivering the project. There may also be contingency allowances to take account of uncertainties. As the project progresses further, more granular cost estimates will be produced and reflected back to the business case budget.

Risks – The longer the timescale of the project, the more difficult it may be to identify the level of uncertainty and the most effective approach. Business case risks are the most important to identify. If they can't be mitigated at this stage it may mean that the project is abandoned or a less risky strategy pursued.

Options appraisal – The strength of any business case is increased when a full range of possible options has been considered. This shows that the organisation has not become over-reliant on a single idea, but that it has reflected on what other options may be possible with the available funds. The do-nothing option may also be considered. When the final business case is ultimately produced, it is approved not only on the basis of being a good idea in itself, but also that in relation to alternatives it was the strongest option. It is common for options to be subject to a financial appraisal considering relative costs in relation to time and the phasing of return value. Options appraisal is a major part of the justification for the chosen option to proceed.

Additional content – As well as the above, the business case may also document information on timeline, success criteria, stakeholders, constraints, assumptions, dependencies and details of any plans.

Role of a project sponsor and project manager in relation to developing a business case

As well as a structured approach to business case development, the views of a number of key stakeholders will also be essential. This will ensure that the business case that has been approved is seen as a realistic proposition by those who may have influence on the resulting project deployment and actual transition of the output into operational use and subsequent benefits realisation.

The following stakeholders may be involved in business case development and contribute to its content:

Project steering group (project board) – The members of the project steering group are often made up of corporate management who, in their monitoring of the organisation's external or internal business environment, have defined a need to consider that change options should be explored.

Project sponsor – Appointed by the steering group and considered to be the owner of the business case, the sponsor will lead its development during the earliest phase of the project. Ultimately the business case may be approved by the steering group and funding released in order that the project proceeds to detailed planning.

Project manager – While there may be a sound business case from a financial point of view, this becomes meaningless if there has been no recognition of how the resultant project is actually going to be managed and delivered. The project manager will be appointed by the sponsor and will contribute detail about the reality of delivering such a change. In some cases, where the project is a smaller internal project within a functional department of the organisation, the project manager may write the business case under the direction of the functional manager (in effect, the sponsor). In this case the project manager may solicit the input of others in the organisation to form the business case content, but it should always be the functional manager who remains accountable for the business case realising the benefits planned.

Other business case contributors

An effective business case results from the consideration of alternative options in addition to the views of stakeholders who may influence either the project output or benefits realisation when the output becomes operable. Other key contributors could be:

Users – They will be key to providing the sponsor with insight about how the output will be operated within business-as-usual. It is their perspective that will add most value to the project and be key to benefits realisation.

Business analyst – This may be an internal role or brought into the organisation as an external consultant, providing a vital link between the project, its stakeholders and both the internal and external environments. A strength of a skilled business analyst is the experience they have gained in other projects and the implementation of these lessons learned in planning a new project.

Subject matter experts – These stakeholders could provide expertise in such areas as procurement, human resources, finance, specific technical areas and process application.

Suppliers – This can sometimes be used as a blanket term when describing some of the roles above. Any stakeholder who has the capacity to input significant detailed knowledge to make the writing of the business case possible and to add value to the decision-making could be considered a supplier.

Taking account of this wide range of contribution can increase the objectivity and stability of a business case throughout the life cycle of the project.

The term 'benefits management'

In most cases a project is initiated in order to deliver change and beneficial outcomes to the sponsoring organisation. The business case documents a detailed account of the decision-making that has underpinned the project to the point where benefits realisation is possible. Benefits management is the identification, definition, planning, tracking and realisation of business benefits.

Benefits realisation is the practice of ensuring that benefits are derived from outputs and outcomes, and is essential to support the achievement of the business case. The business case should contain detail of the upfront plan for any supplemental activities and additional considerations necessary in order for the project output to be in the optimal state for benefits realisation to be possible. The income expected and any operational costs connected to additional activities, including capital expenditure, should also be considered.

During the investment appraisal of project options, the business case for the project depends on stakeholders, such as business change managers, reflecting enough to accurately attribute benefits at the right level – avoiding aspects that yield value being missed or 'double-counted'.

A benefits management plan ensures that there is a proactive management approach to maintain a focus on benefits-driven change throughout the entire life of the project.

Think about...

a project you are familiar with or one that you may have researched and write down five benefits that you would expect to find noted in the business case for that project.

2.1.5 Project life cycles

Learning objectives

This section introduces life cycles, which are fundamental to the management of any project. Organisations will often set a standard approach for project delivery, depending on the desired outputs, benefits and outcomes that are expected.

By the time you have studied this section you will have completed the following:

Learning outcome	Assessment criteria
2 Understand project life cycles	2.1 State the phases of a typical linear project life cycle
	2.2 State the phases of a typical iterative project life cycle
	2.3 Define the term 'hybrid life cycle'
	2.4 Define the term 'extended project life cycle'

Whatever life cycle is chosen, it will provide a structure for governing the progression of the work by acting as an important management tool. It will allow focus on the allocation of resources, the integration of activities, the availability of key individuals, the support of timely decision-making and the mitigation of risk. Additionally, the life cycle also allows the provision of control and governance mechanisms matching the life cycle structure. Consequently, it is important that sponsors and project managers understand the characteristics and specific features of the selected approach.

Approaches to deployment range between highly predictive and highly adaptive settings. The choice between predictive and adaptive philosophies is largely influenced by the availability of knowledge. More predictive approaches tend to rely on knowledge identified at the start, allowing work to proceed in a sequential manner, while adaptive contexts imply that new knowledge is created as the work progresses, which is then used to inform and guide the remaining effort. Adaptive approaches allow more key stakeholders to contribute and shape the development process.

Phases of a typical linear project life cycle

A project progresses through a sequential series of steps, known as phases, from start to finish as shown in Figure 2.1.5.1. Each phase provides only partial capability until the final desired state is reached, usually at the end of the last phase. This is suitable for stable, low-risk environments. When the project scope is defined the phases may be subdivided into smaller elements within the timeline, referred to as stages.

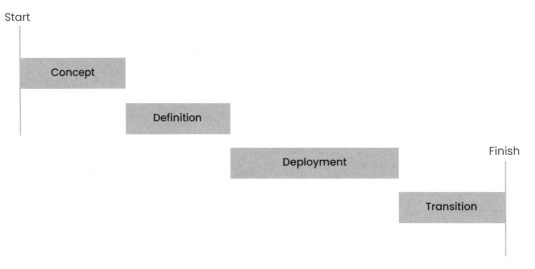

Figure 2.1.5.1 Linear project life cycle

A typical linear life cycle encompasses multiple phases:

Concept – Development of an initial idea through initial studies and high-level requirements management, and assessment of viability, including an outline business case.

Definition – Development of a detailed definition, plans and statement of requirements that include a full justification for the work. It would be typical for a project management plan to form the output of this phase.

Deployment – Implementation of plans and verification of performance through testing and assurance to realise intended outputs, outcomes and benefits.

Transition – Handover, commissioning and acceptance of outputs to the sponsor and wider users, culminating in formal closure.

The linear approach aims to be highly structured, predictable and stable, providing a transparent format for managing contracts and allowing maximum control and governance over the process. It works particularly well for undertaking the delivery of well-understood and clearly defined outputs, trading time, cost and risk to achieve the right scope and quality.

On the other hand, it assumes the availability of relatively perfect knowledge upfront, while being resistant to change and inflexible in terms of corrections and rework. It also implies a long sequence, culminating in the ultimate handover. Dividing knowledge into distinct phases in this way can often create silos and knowledge barriers between the phases, particularly when different delivery agents will deliver different phases. Those carrying out work in the deployment phase may have a tendency to blame activity in the previous phase for any problems they encounter while delivering their assigned workload. In addition, they may have very little incentive to pass on learning to help those delivering pieces of work further on in deployment.

Phases of a typical iterative project life cycle

Iterative project life cycles are most commonly used in agile development projects. Agile is a family of development methodologies where requirements and solutions are developed iteratively and incrementally throughout the life cycle. The life cycle used in an agile approach is composed of several iterations allowing the deployment of initial capability, followed by successive deliveries of further value. They are based on the idea of concurrency, or simultaneous engineering, where different development steps are performed in parallel. Iterative life cycles repeat one or more of the phases before proceeding to the next one, and manage uncertainty regarding the scope by allowing the objectives to evolve throughout the life cycle as learning and discovery take place. Prototypes, timeboxes or parallel activities are used to acquire new insights, obtain feedback or explore high-risk options. The scope of this activity depends on the level of uncertainty and the organisational appetite for risk. The duration may extend throughout deployment.

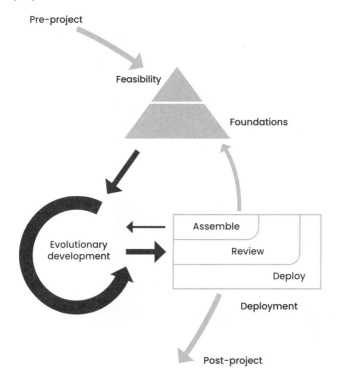

Figure 2.1.5.2 Iterative development in dynamic, agile context

Source: DSDM Agile Project Framework Handbook, 2014

There are six phases in an iterative life cycle and these are shown in Figure 2.1.5.2. During the 'pre-project' phase, iterative life cycles begin by developing a high-level vision. The 'feasibility' and 'foundation' phases ensure that the finer detail is uncovered during the cycles of iteration. The 'evolutionary development' phase allows the specification and design to run in parallel and so it 'fast-tracks' to 'deployment'. Iterations are thus used to progressively elaborate and improve understanding based on client interaction with learning between the iterations. Iterations are applied when the goals are clear but the means of achieving them are not. The rapid deployment of smaller, partial solutions becomes the basis for gaining fast feedback and new insights about what needs to be done. Iterations are often conducted through working prototypes that stakeholders use as the basis for adaptation and improvement. The 'deployment' phase seeks to bring the evolving solution into operational use either fully or using an incremental solution that delivers partial requirements, using user experience to form the next solution increments. The final phase, 'post-project', identifies whether the solution has delivered the benefits to the degree required to achieve the business case.

Overall, using iterations allows earlier return on some of the benefits that have already been implemented while validating the concepts and engaging users.

The term 'hybrid life cycle'

There is no single life cycle model that would suit all applications. The choice is dependent on what the organisation is trying to achieve and what aspects of the project are important. Hybrid life cycles, therefore, enable a pragmatic mix of approaches, typically fusing together elements from predictive and adaptive perspectives to create a new model or approach. For example, using iterative or agile methods for early requirements gathering, where the uncertainty is greatest, and following it up with incremental or sequential processes, derived from the two previously mentioned life cycle models, to formalise deployment, as shown in Figure 2.1.5.3.

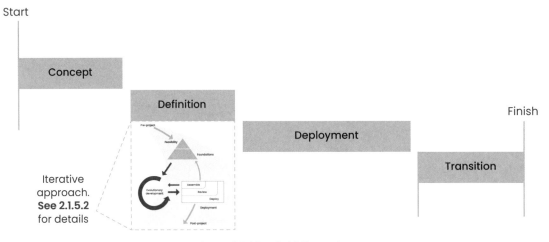

Figure 2.1.5.3 Hybrid life cycle

The use of prototyping, timeboxing or iterative thinking offers tested methods for experimentation and risk reduction.

Adding iterative elements to 'predictive' projects can enhance deployment in stages, support the generation of insights, underpin the realisation of an early benefit stream and validate some of the ideas much earlier in the cycle. Blending, merging or mashing of life cycles, ideas, principles, practices and methods can apply equally to programmes and portfolios. Building agile working into a project or programme can offer increased efficiency and flexibility. However, it also requires great skill and clarity when using multiple different systems of working.

The term 'extended life cycle'

Depending on the particular scope of a project and what it is delivering, the life cycle chosen can present a number of considerations. Some projects will be part of a programme and will be concerned with coordinating the delivery of multiple outputs. Some projects will work as stand-alone projects and would be primarily concerned with delivering their outputs only. Other projects will be expected to incorporate the management of change and the realisation of benefits, and hence require a greatly extended life cycle, as shown in Figure 2.1.5.4. Where a contractor is working for a client, the contractor's 'project' may simply be the deployment and transition phases of the client's project and will include the capability for benefits realisation. In these circumstances the client is responsible for operating the outcomes in a manner that will obtain the desired benefits. In this case the host organisation must ensure attention is given not only to managing the project to closure but also focusing attention on the operational phases, effectively extending the life cycle.

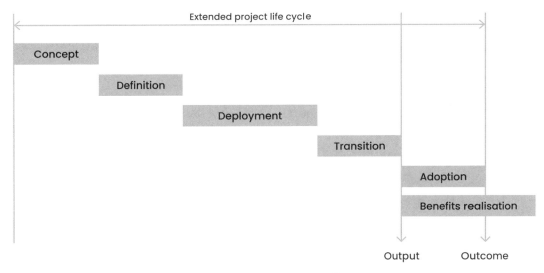

Figure 2.1.5.4 Extended life cycle

Extended life cycles ensure that accountability and governance of the investment stays with a single organisation until the change is fully embedded by offering the missing connection to benefits realisation, while preventing the formation of knowledge boundaries between project teams and operations.

Recognising that many projects are initiated in order to deliver change and beneficial outcomes to organisations, life cycles can incorporate a further phase named 'benefits realisation' that may proceed up to the achievement of the business case.

An additional underpinning phase is also required in order to realise benefits as new outputs need to be made available and accessible to potential users. This may need to be enabled and operated separately. The additional activities included in the extended life cycle encompass:

Adoption – Operations and sustainment required to utilise the new project and enable the acceptance and use of the benefits.

Benefits realisation – Realisation of the required business benefits.

The principal implication of extending the end of the life cycle to incorporate benefits realisation is that there is a need to start upfront, planning for the supplemental activities and incorporating additional considerations during the concept and definition phases. There are income and operational costs connected to the additional activities, as well as spending capital expenditure considerations, which will be addressed during the concept and definition phases.

2.1.6 Project management plan

Learning objectives

This section considers the output of a process of integrated planning for a project and documents this detail in the project management plan (PMP). At this stage the fundamental management components of scope, schedule, cost, risk, quality and resources will be defined. The project manager owns the PMP.

By the time you have studied this section you will have completed the following:

Learning outcome	Assessment criteria
4 Understand project management planning	**4.1** Define the term 'deployment baseline'
	4.2 State how deployment baselines differ between linear and iterative life cycles
	4.3 Outline the stakeholders of a project management plan
	4.10 Explain why establishing success criteria is important at the start of during and at handover of a project

The term 'deployment baseline'

Once all of the management components have been planned and integrated this will form the deployment baseline, which is approved, along with the PMP, at the decision gate associated with the approval of significant project costs. Some projects may have an integrated baseline review to provide assurance prior to approval. The approval of the deployment baseline is a good time to reconfirm the boundaries of the project – both what is in and out of scope, and how the project interfaces with other projects or business-as-usual activities in a programme or strategic portfolio. Some areas may require a rework of the integrated plan prior to approval – either to adjust scope or to make provision for a different amount of cost contingency to take account of exposure to risks, and to fund risk responses that are not built into core scope.

The project can then proceed to the deployment phase, where the deployment baseline will be used for monitoring progress and implementing change control.

The deployment baseline in linear and iterative life cycles

Depending on particular project objectives and the life cycle chosen, different approaches to planning time, resources and cost, in the context of risk, can be adopted.

When using a linear life cycle approach, the assumption underpinning integrated planning is that all the work can be defined, estimated, scheduled, resourced and costed, and associated risks can be assessed. This may be done to different levels of granularity in the near term and the long term; nevertheless, a management baseline can be established from which deployment can be managed and controlled, and the value expectations are then understood for the whole project. Unexpected issues will inevitably arise during deployment, but this does not negate the need for the best plan possible before work starts.

When using an iterative life cycle approach, a baseline plan is still required, but the assumptions underpinning the plan are different, with flexibility and agility built into the thinking. In an iterative project life cycle, the baseline resources and schedule are determined, but the achievement of scope and quality may vary from the plan as teams may have autonomy to re-prioritise tasks and act on new knowledge. Any work not achieved in the time allocated is returned to an existing backlog allowance, to then be planned into the future schedule or removed from the project.

Linear life cycles treat scope and quality as the driver and calculate the consequential consumed time and cost. Iterative projects commit to set resources over limited periods to deliver products that are developed over successive cycles. Many organisations use a hybrid linear/iterative approach to projects and programmes most of the time. The challenge is to plan in the most effective way to give the investing organisation the best possible chance of achieving the objectives and benefits described in the business case.

The stakeholders of a project management plan

The PMP is the consolidated plan for the project and, as such, communicates the details of the approved project plans to stakeholders. It has been produced through a facilitated exercise led by the project manager, with the engagement of all key stakeholders who will be involved in the deployment of the project, and will act as a reference source for all other stakeholders as shown in Figure 2.1.6.1.

It is important to have as much continuity as possible throughout deployment. Achieving this can often be difficult, particularly if the project resources are procured under a specific contract and are not considered to be employed staff. In circumstances like these there can often be a large amount of staff turnover. This transient flow of resources should not adversely affect the project if the PMP is available, up to date and used as a major part of the induction material for new members of the team.

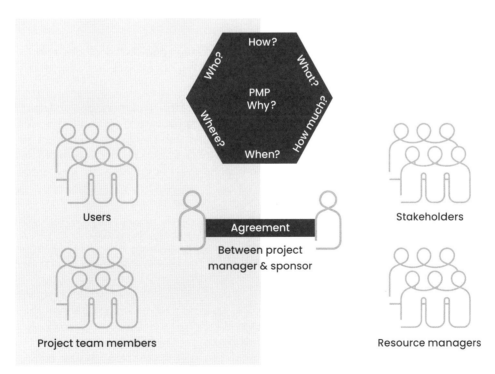

Figure 2.1.6.1 Different stakeholders that may need to contribute to producing the PMP

The PMP is often referred to as the 'contract' between the project manager and the sponsor and, as such, clearly illustrates the extent of that agreement. It is important for the project manager to fully understand what is expected of them prior to committing to deployment. The PMP acts as a valuable source of clarification in this respect. It is important when conducting gate reviews that the current PMP is used as a reference source.

Typical contents of a project management plan

In essence the PMP should answer the 'why?', 'what?', 'when?', 'who?', 'where?' and 'how?' of the project. The 'how much?' question may also be asked. The size of the project will influence the size of the PMP, which may run into several volumes, for example, for the construction of a large nuclear power station, but may only be several pages for a small, simple internal project.

Why? This question has already been answered by the business case. The PMP will therefore reference details from the business case, which can act as an appendix to the PMP.

What? This contains a specific description of the scope of the project in the first instance and then becomes more refined as the project nears deployment. Also contained here are details of the acceptance criteria and any important constraints.

When? The timeline will be outlined here together with various supporting documentation such as a Gantt chart and project life cycle approach.

Who? The organisation breakdown structure (OBS) will be shown here together with responsibility assignments, reporting lines and role descriptions.

How much? This considers the budget presented as a cost breakdown structure (CBS) showing how the budget has been allocated to the work. It is likely that the cash flow for the project will be presented in the form of a spending projection for the project duration.

Where? This presents the logistics of the project location and site conditions, and outlines any major restrictions or constraints regarding access, or particular delivery requirements and security protocols.

How? This is probably the most comprehensive part of the document, and outlines the management strategy for the project. These management plans will contain process steps, template documents, roles and responsibilities, communication requirements and the detailed information necessary to allow those involved in deployment to follow the required process. Specific management plans could exist for the following areas:

- risk
- quality
- procurement
- stakeholders and communication
- safety
- scope
- change control procedures
- cost
- project controls
- information

This information, when assembled in a self-contained document, is now a standard reference for all concerned with the project. The list given may not all be applicable to every project but represents common examples of content.

The importance of establishing success criteria at the start of during and at the handover of a project

Project success is the satisfaction of stakeholder needs and is measured by the success criteria agreed at the start of a project. All projects are designed to bring benefits to the investing organisation, but the success criteria for many projects exclude benefits realisation, as this is handled by another part of the organisation.

Success criteria are agreed with stakeholders as early as possible but can be changed at any time in the project life cycle, subject to approval through change control. In an iterative working environment, the team may find it easier to respond to changing success criteria, as they deliver and regularly test outputs with end users, allowing for gradual learning and adaptation.

The degree of achievement of project management success criteria will be known at project handover, and accountability for achieving the project success criteria rests with the project manager. Benefits are often realised some time after transition into use, hence accountability for benefits realisation rests with the sponsor.

Think about...

a project you are familiar with or one that you may have researched and write down five frameworks or policies you would expect to find in the PMP for that project.

2.2 Planning for success

Section 2.1 identified the high-level expressions of stakeholder vision. It is now necessary to consider just how that need is likely to be delivered through to a detailed statement of work for the chosen solution. This continuation of the journey involves a number of steps of refinement: exploring objectives, detailed requirements, success criteria, measurable benefits, best-value options, scope definition and acceptance criteria for each element of that scope. This work builds a firm foundation for detailed planning.

The linear progression from high-level expressions of need and benefit in an early business case through to the specification of detailed requirements, scope and acceptance criteria is well understood. For many projects, this remains a value-creating process, especially for large-scale, highly technical projects, where rework is expensive and does not justify an iterative approach.

The emergence and growing popularity of iterative approaches requires project managers to think about defining outputs in a different, more adaptive way. The danger, however, is to assume that the approaches designed to build in agility and flexibility do not require the discipline to define some things clearly, for example, benefits that justify the investment or the acceptance criteria for deliverables.

Taking forward the definition of outputs into detailed planning requires a focus on multiple areas, the success of which is dependent on the integration of those areas into the baseline project management plan. Depending on particular project objectives and the life cycle chosen, different approaches to planning time, resources and cost, in the context of risk, can be adopted.

Stakeholders – those individuals or groups who have an interest or role in the project, programme or portfolio, or are impacted by it – cannot by definition be 'managed'. Rather, depending on their stake, and the role that they will ideally play, the people involved in the work, from sponsor to team member, are part of the effort to keep the stakeholder appropriately engaged and influenced to do the right things. This is not an easy task and benefits from a facilitative approach rather than assuming that 'command-and-control' approaches will be effective.

This section continues the learning journey and includes:

2.2.1 **Stakeholder engagement**

2.2.2 **Communication**

2.2.3 **Risk and issue management**

2.2.4 **Quality management**

2.2.5 **Scope management**

2.2.1 Stakeholder engagement

Learning objectives

This section considers those who ultimately will be key to the project's success: stakeholders. Without the effective engagement of stakeholders there is a risk that the project will not meet its success criteria.

By the time you have studied this section you will have completed the following:

Learning outcome	Assessment criteria
4 Understand project management planning	**4.6** Explain how a stakeholder analysis supports effective stakeholder engagement

Stakeholders are people, groups or institutions with interests in a programme or project. Primary stakeholders are immediate communities of interest; often they will be described as internal stakeholders, particularly if they are involved directly with the implementation of the project. Secondary stakeholders (usually external stakeholders) are the intermediaries in the process, and may include government agencies and other institutional bodies.

Groups or individuals closest to the project may not actually think of themselves as stakeholders, because they feel they own the management processes, for example, the project manager and team. A rule of thumb for ensuring that key stakeholders have been included in the process is to question whose support or lack of it might significantly influence the success of the project. This is a particularly good test where groups claim to speak for a wider representation than may be the case, and their capacity to articulate their concerns might easily cause other groups to be overlooked.

Stakeholder analysis supporting effective stakeholder engagement

If our ultimate goal is stakeholder engagement, we first need to look at each stakeholder and their relationship to the project. Different types of relationships need different kinds of approaches; some need more activity than others. Similarly, stakeholders can be quite specific, for example, as individuals or geographically identifiable groups of people, while others are more difficult to define and we have to think more laterally about how we are going to establish and maintain a relationship with them.

Stakeholder analysis starts with the identification of a project's key stakeholders, and assessing their interests in the project and the ways in which those interests affect project risks and viability. It contributes to project design by identifying the goals and roles of different groups, and by helping to formulate appropriate forms of engagement with these groups. Developing a sound stakeholder environment means understanding the needs of stakeholders, both perceived and in reality. A typical approach could include:

- understanding the roles of the various stakeholders, and how this information may be used as an opportunity to improve both the perception and reception of the project
- identifying the real nature of each stakeholder group's business and their consequent interest in the project
- understanding stakeholders' behaviours and motivations towards the project
- assessing how stakeholders may react to various approaches and methods of communication

- identifying the characteristics of the stakeholders' environments and developing appropriate responses to facilitate a good relationship
- responding to the stakeholders' motivations in relation to the project
- determining the key areas that will have the most impact on the successful reception of the project

Ultimately project management must take into consideration all parties whose actions may change the course of the project. The objectives of these stakeholders involved in a project are unlikely to be congruent, for example, the aim of the sponsoring organisation is to minimise the cost of the project and that of the delivery contractor is to maximise profit. Project managers should be aware of all stakeholders and their likely objectives. They will find it difficult to please all of them because the objectives are often in conflict. Political skill will be a useful attribute to assure maximum satisfaction among the stakeholders.

Environmental groups are perhaps a good example of stakeholders who often have a direct and categoric opposition to the project, regardless of how it is eventually implemented. For example, the decision on whether to build Terminal 5 at Heathrow Airport, London, was held up for more than 10 years by stakeholders influencing one of the most complex public inquiries ever mounted in Britain.

Having identified the various stakeholders, each may be assigned to a category according to their relative ability to influence the project and the level of power they are thought to have. Figure 2.2.1.1 shows a typical power–interest matrix used to position stakeholders accordingly. Three distinct tasks are envisaged, namely:

- identification and mapping of relevant stakeholders
- analysis of their interests in and relative power over the project or programme
- development of an outline action plan defining how each stakeholder group will be managed throughout the life cycle of the project and the likelihood of them supporting the project

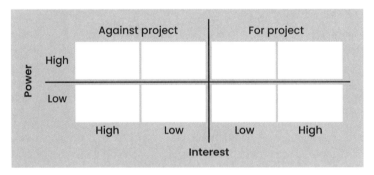

Figure 2.2.1.1 An approach to capturing analysis of stakeholders

Power is a factor that is related to influence. Each stakeholder is analysed as to their degree of importance according to their level of power and therefore their ability to influence the project. Appropriate members of the project team can then prioritise their efforts accordingly to maintain the necessary stakeholder engagement, thus giving rise to the best chances of ultimate project success. If the project is large enough, or the stakeholder linkages are sufficiently intense, the project team's stakeholder engagement efforts may be assigned to a specific group within the project team. Assignments of this kind would be fully recorded in the project's communication plan. This plan will assign specific responsibilities to those who will conduct communication, and describe the overall engagement strategy of how information about the project will be conveyed to those who need that information, who could be external stakeholders, such as the general public, for example.

Carrying out such an in-depth analysis of stakeholders will consume resources, and so to justify this consumption the project manager must acknowledge the importance of managing stakeholder expectations and how they will influence the overall success of the project, particularly in the areas described below.

Improved communications planning

Not everybody needs to know everything, but everybody needs to know something. The results of the analysis will define the key communication requirements. These requirements are essential to assure effective engagement. This is especially true if the key interests of the stakeholders have been gathered in terms of time, cost, quality, scope and benefits. Not only can the appropriate level of information be ascertained, but also where the information will come from and how it will be transmitted.

Ensuring a productive team is formed

Knowing which is the most appropriate engagement strategy to adopt for stakeholders – either partnering, being consultative or needing to be involved or simply kept informed – will help to define whether or not they need a place on the team. The outputs of the analysis should indicate which stakeholder relationships might be most productive for the project being considered. Those seen as partners may play a key role as suppliers and members of the steering group, depending on their interests and level of seniority. Engagement strategies for stakeholders in other areas may ultimately encourage them to be partners too. Similarly, if there are many stakeholder groups that need to be consulted, this may mean that a team needs to be formed to complete these activities.

Enabling effective engagement actions to be initiated

Once identified, it is possible to apply a further analysis to the stakeholders to develop an engagement strategy for dealing with them. Effective engagement requires the project team to focus on understanding stakeholder perspectives and to address these in order to achieve the intended outcomes. Putting in effort to explore stakeholder points of view has the dual benefit of building understanding of the issues and building relationships.

Increased likelihood of project being accepted

There are stakeholders who are important, particularly when the project reaches the handover, as they will decide whether the output should be accepted or not. Identifying these stakeholders from the outset and fulfilling their needs will be a big step in ensuring stakeholder satisfaction is sufficient to warrant the product being accepted into the operational environment.

2.2.2 Communication

Learning objectives

This section considers how communication should be conducted if the project is to successfully take account of stakeholders' requirements. There are different communication methods to be considered and documented in a communication plan for the project.

By the time you have studied this section you will have completed the following:

Learning outcome	Assessment criteria
9. Understand communication in the context of a project	9.1 Define the term 'communication'
	9.2 Outline the advantages of different communication methods (including face-to-face, physical and virtual)
	9.3 Outline the disadvantages of different communication methods (including face-to-face, physical and virtual)
	9.4 Outline the contents of a communication plan
	9.5 Explain the benefits, to a project manager, of a communication plan

The term 'communication'

Communication is the process of exchanging information and confirming there is shared understanding. The ability to communicate is a core skill for people working in projects: to ensure objectives and requirements are understood, plans and benefits are shared, stakeholders are aligned, teams are motivated and knowledge is embedded.

Advantages and disadvantages of different communication methods

Communication takes many forms and effective communicators consider not only the message they want to pass on, but also the method (medium) for communicating the message. Decisions about communication methods are made in the context of the target audience, the intended impact and the risks/potential unintended consequences of the approach.

Many factors affect the success of communication, from cultural influences to the 'mood' in the team to the method of communication chosen and the language used. Project professionals can choose to use written words and symbols, voice and non-verbal signals (including body language) when communicating. In 'face-to-face' communication (including video and vlogs), non-verbal communication can have more of an impact than the words used, so being able to control non-verbal signals and create a coherent message is vital.

Where face-to-face communication is not possible there are advantages and disadvantages. For example, it can be advantageous to be on a conference call if the group is working through feedback in a document as more focus can be given to the words used and the format of the written information without worrying about visual clues. A disadvantage is that virtual communication runs the risk of the sentiment underpinning what is said being misunderstood.

Physical (non-verbal) communication includes facial expressions, the tone and pitch of the voice, and gestures displayed through body language. Symbols, signs and gestures can also be regarded as physical communication skills. An advantage of physical communication is that important communication messages can be emphasised by aspects such as facial expressions and the variations in the tone and pitch of the voice. A disadvantage of this type of communication is that the recipient may misinterpret the communication clues, leading to the wrong message being conveyed. Different cultures also have different ways of interpreting physical communication. There have been a number of cases where a communication sign has been used to convey a positive message only to be received by different culture as a grave insult. Care should be taken to fully understand the extent of use of physical communication and ensuring that the message conveyed is in fact the message that is most likely to be received.

If the project requires working with virtual teams there are particular skills needed to ensure that communication between team members is efficient and effective, for example, the ability to include everyone who needs to be involved on a virtual call, simultaneously.

The contents of a communication plan

An effective communication plan will seek to form an engagement strategy, as a result of suitable analysis, by answering some of the following questions:

- What particular message(s) should be communicated to this particular stakeholder?
- Who, in the project organisation, is best placed to carry out this communication?
- What form of message medium or method will motivate this stakeholder to engage the most?
- When and how often should communication take place?
- What form of feedback can be solicited or expected?
- What barriers can be proactively identified and acted upon prior to communication taking place?
- Which stakeholders should/should not communicate with each other?

The communication plan allows the essential interactions to take place that are deemed necessary to motivate those stakeholders whose support is needed to achieve the desired outcomes. Putting in effort to analyse stakeholders' points of view has the dual benefit of building understanding of the issues and developing positive relationships. Managing stakeholders' influence relies on these relationships being maintained and can only realistically be achieved through having an effective communications plan.

Benefits, to a project manager, of a communication plan

Effective communication plans include ways to receive feedback and measure effectiveness so that plans can be adjusted to have maximum impact. Taking the time to develop an effective communication plan will yield the following benefits:

- **The most appropriate communication medium is used** – Choosing the most appropriate medium for delivery of a message is vital to that message being received and understood by stakeholders. The communication plan will consider which medium is best for which situation and stakeholder. For example, avoiding over-reliance on electronic forms of communication, which can lead to misunderstanding and conflict.

- **More focused communication to stakeholders** – Avoiding mass communication, where receivers are swamped with information, only some of which might be relevant to them. Instead, messages are planned and tailored to convey the communicator's meaning as accurately as possible to the target audience. If the right information is provided at the right time, messages are then more likely to be read by the intended recipients.

- **More consistent communication** – When communication is planned in advance all messages will be delivered using a framework that has been agreed and approved. This could, for example, involve the assigning of specific responsibilities for communication in the project. The result is that stakeholders do not receive conflicting messages from different areas of the project.

- **Communication can be systematically improved** – By ensuring that free-flowing feedback channels are planned into the communication structure, communication barriers can be identified, allowing improvement actions to be proactively taken to ensure that barriers are eliminated and communication can be conducted more effectively.

- **Greater adherence to the organisation's governance and standards** – It is important to adhere to any protocols or standards for communication that are developed in the organisation for effective communication to take place. The communication plan will take account of any 'norms' in the particular organisation and so circumvent avoidable communication errors, potential conflict or security breaches.

Understanding how communication can be affected by a range of factors will ensure that the project manager seeks to proactively manage these factors as much as possible prior to the communication taking place. By doing this, the communication plan for the project will increase the chances of achieving effective engagement, which in turn improves the chance of achieving objectives by having a positive influence on stakeholders' behaviours.

Think about...

a situation where communication was required. Was the exchange successful? Write below what made it successful and what could have been done to improve the communication opportunity.

Factors leading to success/failure	Improvement ideas

Read about... The world of project management

Nuclear decommissioning agent Sellafield Ltd has used effective communication planning when communicating a positive message to attract the best talent to fulfil its task to deal with the nuclear waste fuel legacy – itself a 100-year decommissioning project in Cumbria – but at the same time reduce Cumbria's dependency on Sellafield as the main employer for the area. Neil Crewdson, head of project management and capabilities at Sellafield, comments on how Honda has implemented a major plant shutdown in Swindon and he draws parallels with Sellafield's current task.

Reskill and invest

Neil says that a priority for the project managers handling the closure is to rebuild some confidence in their mission of finishing the production of the Honda Civic, and to see it out with pride. "We did something similar," he says. "A large part of Sellafield was about reprocessing, and that's been the business for the last 50 years. The first plant shut down last year, and we tried to instil a sense of 'finishing our mission with pride'."

But, Crewdson says, "It is easier for us at Sellafield because, for the next 10 to 20 years, we don't foresee any redundancies. What we do see is a massive reskilling and retraining programme, and help finding employment and weaning the area off Sellafield. When we've faced downturns, we've done recruitment days for all large industries that want our skills."

Sellafield expects gradual reduction in 20 years' time and is already investing in developing new facilities in the local community to house and encourage new start-ups and entrepreneurial businesses.

In terms of handling the media, Crewdson says Sellafield now prefers to enlist the help of advocates – such as Sellafield's apprentices – to talk about the site, rather than using nuclear industry experts to get their messages across. "People don't trust people in white coats any more; they moved away from deferring to experts."

It also pays to be open in communicating with the national media. "We really try to be very transparent," Crewdson says.

Originally published in *Project* Summer 2019.

If you would like to read more about this example or other real-world project examples, copies of APM's *Project* journal can be downloaded from the members' resources area of the APM website: apm.org.uk/project.

2.2.3 Risk and issue management

Learning objectives

This section examines two of the most misunderstood of all the project management processes: risk management and issue management. Understanding risk management means that the project can exploit the existing opportunities to further optimise the project schedule, budget and scope. Issues are events where, in effect, the project is caught by surprise and needs to respond. Issues may not be avoidable but what is important is that the process applied to deal with such eventualities creates valuable lessons learned.

By the time you have studied this section you will have completed the following:

Learning outcome	Assessment criteria
7 Understand project risk and issue management in the context of a project	**7.1** Define the term 'risk'
	7.2 Explain the purpose of risk management
	7.3 Outline the stages of a typical risk management process (including identification, analysis, response and closure)
	7.4 Describe the use of risk registers
	7.5 Define the term 'issue'
	7.6 Outline the purpose of issue management
	7.7 Differentiate between an issue and a risk
	7.8 State the stages of an issue resolution process

The term 'risk'

Risk is the potential of a situation or event to impact on the achievement of specific objectives. It is the level of uncertainty that exists. This is not a negative thing as long as the project is aware that uncertainty exists and can proactively consider the best way to respond to that uncertainty.

The purpose of risk management

Risk management is a process that allows individual risk events and overall risk to be understood and managed proactively, optimising success by minimising threats and maximising opportunities.

All projects are inherently risky because they are unique, constrained, based on assumptions, performed by people and subject to external influences. Risks can affect the achievement of objectives either positively or negatively. Risk includes both opportunities and threats, and both should be managed through the risk management process.

Risk management must be closely aligned to schedule management. Cost, time and resource estimates should always take risks into account. The project manager is accountable for ensuring that risk management takes place. Depending on the size and complexity of the project, a specialist risk manager may be appointed to oversee and facilitate the risk management process.

A typical risk management process

It is important to note that the risk management process discussed here is not applied to the management of general health and safety risks, which are usually excluded from project risk management. Management of these risks is traditionally handled separately through the formation of a safety plan for the project, often with the support of the health and safety function within the organisation. The process of project risk management will focus on individual project risks that, should they occur, will affect the project's objectives. The project manager will also seek to understand the overall risk exposure of the project, so that this can be reported to the project sponsor and other stakeholders. A typical risk management process is illustrated in Figure 2.2.3.1.

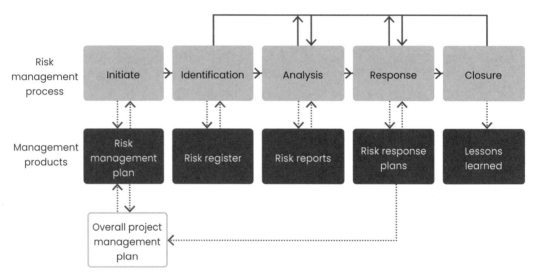

Figure 2.2.3.1 Risk management process and management products

The steps are as follows:

Initiate – The main purpose of this step is to ensure that there is a common understanding of the project to which the risk management process is to be applied. It is important that risk management is not seen by the project team as a burdensome process that will ensure every box is ticked. Instead, this step will make sure that the level of process to be used fits the specific requirements of the project.

A key output from the initiation step is the risk management plan, which details how risk will be managed throughout the life cycle. The risk management plan will be an important reference for all stakeholders who require an insight into the risk organisation and control structure, and the specific responsibilities for risk management. A number of appendices will also be included, such as templates and proformas of the documents necessary to effectively carry out the process. Part of the overall project management plan, the risk management plan makes it quite clear how risk is going to be tackled for the project. In many organisations it may be held as a template in the standard project methodology, although the risk management plan will always be specific to a particular project.

Identification – The objective of risk identification is to draw out all knowable risks to project objectives. Risk identification is a creative, divergent process that benefits from the input of a wide range of people using a method that does not restrict or bias their thinking. Working with stakeholders and the team to discuss risk is one area that requires a facilitative approach and a means of providing neutral challenges to address any bias. Workshops are often used for this purpose, although alternative approaches that enable individuals to contribute without any chance of group bias can be more useful.

To make sense of differing perceptions, it is important to describe risk events clearly, separating causes (facts now or stable planning assumptions), from risk events (situations that may occur) and effects (that have an impact on one or more of the project-specific scales already defined). Once risks are identified they are documented in the risk register.

It is also vital that the correct risk owner is defined for each risk event at this stage in the risk management process. Risk owners are individuals or groups who are best placed to assess and manage the specific risk. Working with the risk owner, the project manager ensures that risks are clearly described in the risk register before moving on to the risk analysis step of the risk management process.

Analysis – The relative severity of identified risks is assessed using qualitative techniques to gain understanding of their individual significance and/or their combined impact on objectives. They can then be prioritised for further attention. Risk owners will work with the project team to carry out basic qualitative analysis as a minimum to identify and prioritise risk events based on an assessment of the:

- probability/likelihood of occurrence
- size of impact on schedule, cost, benefits and potentially other objectives

Response – The risk owner uses information collected during risk identification and risk analysis to advise the project manager whether it makes sense to proactively invest previously unplanned time and money to bring the exposure to risk within acceptable levels. The decision on when to take the risk or invest in increasing certainty is influenced by the appetite for risk of the sponsor and ultimately the investing organisation.

If there is a justification for investing time and money proactively to increase certainty, the project manager makes provision to implement the planned responses (time, resource, cost) and updates the integrated project plan (deployment baseline) accordingly.

Closure – The final part of the management process is to ensure that all risks are closed when they have occurred, they have been successfully mitigated or accepted, or there is no longer a possibility of them occurring. At this stage it is useful to document information about the risk being closed, for example, any updated risk information, closure rationale and lessons learned. There are valuable benefits in fully understanding a risk, the approach to analysis, how it was mitigated or what conditions have been met when closing a risk, for future reference.

At project closure if there are any open risks remaining, the project manager must ensure that these are communicated to those involved in the adoption phase.

The use of risk registers

A risk register is a document listing identified risk events and their corresponding planned responses. The term 'risk log' is also used to describe such a document. It provides a standard format in which to record risk information. As a minimum, for each risk this information is likely to include the description, causes, probability, impact, mitigation actions, fallbacks and status, and the names of individuals with responsibility for the risk's management. Depending on the risk management techniques selected, other data is also likely to be maintained, as appropriate.

Although a risk register can be maintained manually, most projects are likely to use spreadsheet software for this purpose. Such spreadsheets may be designed for a stand-alone PC or for concurrent use by users linked through a network.

The term 'issue'

An issue is a problem that is now breaching, or is about to breach, delegated tolerances for work on a project or programme. These tolerances represent the degree of variability that the project sponsor is willing to accept with regard to the project's performance in reaching its time, cost and quality objectives. Issues require support from the sponsor to agree a resolution. Issues are differentiated from problems that may be escalated from the team to the project manager and dealt with on a day-to-day basis. It is possible that these problems could in fact be issues and require onward escalation to the sponsor, but such an eventuality should be considered rare.

The purpose of issue management

The purpose of issue management is to provide a common process that can be used to identify and document those issues that have occurred and apply an appropriate resolution plan. Issue management plays an important role in maintaining project stability and efficiency throughout the deployment of the project. At the end of the project the information documented from the issue register will be used to provide valuable lessons learned when planning future projects.

Differentiating between an issue and risk

There is often a tendency to mix up the identification, analysis and management of risks with issues. They are related but are not the same thing. Issues may develop when particular risks or groups of risks actually occur and the mitigation actions that have been put in place to deal with these risks are insufficient to such a degree that it requires escalation to the next level of management for resolution. If risks occur and the contingencies that have been reserved are consumed to the expected degree, then that is not an issue. Issues that are happening may also be causes of new risks, or result in the assessment of risk likelihood and/or size of impact to change. It is understandable that a project manager might prioritise the management of issues (problems now) over the management of risks (potential problems or opportunities), but a project where this is continually the case would suggest an underlying concern with project plans and controls.

The stages of an issue resolution process

The process used to resolve issues ensures the following:

- When an issue is identified it is logged in an issue register/log and analysis is performed quickly to understand the nature of the issue, its causes, and its impacts if it is not resolved. The prioritisation of issues is based on the impact on success criteria and benefits for the work, taking into account the relative priorities of scope, quality, time, cost and benefits in the business case.
- Issues are escalated to the sponsor, who may, in turn, escalate them to the governance board for resolution.
- Actions are assigned to the person or group who is best placed to address the issue and identify and implement a resolution in a timely manner.
- Issues that result in changes to scope or any other part of the baseline plan are progressed through change control. As part of integrated planning, the limits of delegated authority are established, and formal change control is required when these tolerances are breached.
- The management of issues is tracked from identification through to resolution, including any change control and replanning of the deployment baseline and project management plan.

Think about...

a project you have researched or may be familiar with and note down some of the steps used to manage risk. Check these steps against the process defined in this section.

Read about... The world of project management

One of the benefits of risk management is that it actually facilitates greater risk-taking. Calculated risk-taking has always been the basis for success. This has to be, of course, within the bounds of applying formal risk management techniques, with appropriate mitigation and fallback plans. Another aspect of risk-taking is risk appetite – how much risk investors are willing to tolerate in achieving their objectives. Pamela Stacey explains a little more of her experiences at HS2, the planned high-speed rail route in the UK.

What's your appetite for risk?

How often does your project team, or its sponsors, actively discuss risk appetite? "Understanding what risks can and can't be taken, and for what rewards, ought to be a much bigger part of project planning," says Pamela Stacey, head of programme and corporate assurance for HS2. "It's a guiding principle. At HS2, safety is our number-one concern – and people might say that makes our risk appetite too low. But it needs to be that way to avoid other priorities displacing it at any point."

The other misconception she has come across is confusion between 'risks' and 'issues'. "The difference is things in the future versus things now," she explains. "People on a project often prefer to address what they can see happening. It feels tangible, and a solution can be found. But they forget that an issue cropping up is just a risk that has crystallised."

Her prescription? Look at what the immediate issues tell you about how risks are developing and might surface in the future. "If you don't have that analysis, you'll struggle to update your risk profile thoroughly. Issues tell stories."

Stacey, who also sits on the committee of APM's Assurance Specific Interest Group, adds: "If you're focused on the next milestone or stage gate, you might stop looking forward at risks that could emerge later – or the overall project outcomes." So, look beyond a post-project 'lessons learned' process – and adapt dynamically to the way risk evolves.

Originally published in *Project* Autumn 2019.

If you would like to read more about this example or other real-world project examples, copies of APM's *Project* journal can be downloaded from the members' resources area of the APM website: apm.org.uk/project.

2.2.4 Quality management

Learning objectives

This section considers the processes necessary to ensure that outputs are delivered in accordance with requirements and have the highest chance of being accepted at the point of final delivery. If the project's stakeholders are satisfied with the results of the project, the project has met its quality criteria.

By the time you have studied this section you will have completed the following:

Learning outcome	Assessment criteria
8 Understand quality in the context of a project	8.1 Define the term 'quality'
	8.2 Outline the purpose of quality management
	8.3 Define the term 'quality planning'
	8.4 Define the term 'quality control'
	8.5 Outline the purpose of quality assurance
	8.6 State the purpose of decision gates, post-project reviews, benefit reviews and project audits

The term 'quality'

Quality is defined as the fitness for purpose or the degree of conformance of the outputs of a process, or the process itself, to requirements.

The purpose of quality management

Quality management is a discipline for ensuring the outputs and benefits, and the processes by which they are delivered, meet stakeholder requirements and are fit for purpose. Project quality management includes the processes required to ensure that the project will satisfy the needs for which it was undertaken. The project quality management system includes all activities of the overall management function that assigns responsibilities for quality and determines the quality objectives, and implements them by means such as quality planning, quality assurance, quality control and continual improvement.

Project quality management must address both the management of the project and the outputs of the project. Failure to meet quality requirements in either dimension can have serious negative effects for some or all of the project stakeholders.

The term 'quality planning'

The starting point for establishing quality in the project is quality planning, which takes the defined scope of the project (or the next phase or time period in an iterative life cycle) and specifies the criteria to be used to validate that the outputs are fit for purpose and acceptable to the sponsor.

As a result of quality planning, the quality plan will be created and is agreed with the sponsor and wider governance board as a key part of the overall project management plan. The quality plan sets out the desired attributes of work in scope and how these are to be assessed. To do this, it references applicable regulations, standards, specifications and, in some cases, values of the investing organisation. Most importantly the quality plan will note the agreed acceptance criteria, in order to provide guidance to the team about the requirements and essential conditions for the deliverable that they are working on. They also guide the planning of quality control and other assurance activities that are performed to check that outputs meet requirements. It is important to do this after scope definition and before any further planning is carried out, as quality control and assurance activities take time and consume resources that need to be scheduled and costed.

The quality plan documents:

- methods of verifying that the outputs meet requirements
- pass/fail criteria for each method
- frequency of the tests, checks or audits that will be carried out
- requirements for resources needed, for example, particular test equipment, suitably qualified and experienced staff who may be provided by the delivery organisation or a part of the supply chain, stakeholder approvals

Obtaining stakeholder agreement facilitates the handover of the project's outputs on completion, and planning early how this will be done is a key success factor for project management.

The term 'quality control'

Quality control consists of inspection, measurement and testing to verify that the project outputs meet the acceptance criteria defined during quality planning. Quality control is focused on preventing problems being passed on to the internal or external customer. For quality control to be effective, change control of specifications and test plans is vital so that any modifications are formally authorised, coordinated and communicated.

As part of quality planning, test plans for quality control will have been agreed. These include aspects such as:

- sample size of tests, for example, the whole item or a percentage chosen at random
- test protocols, including resources required – people, equipment – third-party expertise or facilities
- independent performance and/or witness testing by a regulator or process owner from business-as-usual

There are many project scenarios where the project outputs are highly complex and technical, and where the work to verify conformance of outputs to specifications is extensive. Testing is well established and understood in these scenarios. It is easy to overlook the fact that all projects need to deliver outputs that are fit for purpose and therefore enable the outcomes to be achieved. Quality control applies equally to interim or final outputs such as reports, processes, communication materials or financial models.

In all quality control activities, decisions need to be made about the degree of conformance of the output (or sample of outputs) tested to the specification and acceptance criteria, and what action to take in the event of non-conformance. Quality control is the least flexible of the processes as the result is pass or fail, whereas with quality assurance the processes could be followed to a degree and still deliver an acceptable output.

Projects deliver a huge variety of outputs and are consequently subject to many forms of quality control depending on the technical nature of the work and the particular requirements of individual industries. The quality control regime for the project is established by the project manager, drawing on input from relevant technical experts, rather than by reference to generic processes.

The purpose of quality assurance

The purpose of quality assurance is to create a process for evaluating overall project performance on a regular basis to provide confidence that the project will satisfy the relevant quality standards. It is a complementary practice, alongside quality planning and control, to assure that project outputs meet requirements.

Quality assurance attempts to build in quality through the consistent use of standard processes and procedures, supported by training and feedback. Quality assurance answers one important question: is the project actually following the processes and procedures as set out in the quality plan? There is no point in consuming resources to form a plan if the project then follows a different route. Quality assurance is always performed through an independent audit, either external to the organisation or at least external to the project.

A summary view of how the main quality processes interact is shown in Figure 2.2.4.1.

Figure 2.2.4.1 Quality management as implemented within the project

The purpose of decision gates, post-project reviews, benefit reviews and project audits

A review is a critical evaluation of a deliverable, business case or project management process. Reviews are one of the principal mechanisms by which the quality of deliverables, the performance of the management process and the ongoing viability of the work are assured.

Decision gates

The purpose of decision gates is to review and confirm viability of the work across the chosen life cycle. In a linear life cycle, decision gates are event-driven, at the end of a phase of work. In the case of an iterative life cycle, they are time bound. Many projects or programmes adopt a hybrid life cycle with a combination of main decision gates at the end of major phases of work, supplemented by interim review points to reflect the iterative nature of the development.

In all cases, the sponsor and the wider governance board are accountable for the decision to continue the work. Reviews in advance of decision gates ask four key questions:

- What has been achieved?
- What is required for the next stage?
- What are the key decisions to be made?
- Is the business case still viable, i.e. can the desired benefits be achieved for an acceptable level of cost and risk?

Within a stand-alone project, the decision gate is dealing only with the continued viability of that project's business case. In programmes and portfolios, decisions will include whether to re-phase or terminate existing, or initiate new, projects. Between decision gates, the sponsor is accountable for ensuring authorities are in place to prevent the team working out of compliance and at risk. Decision gates may also be used to request relevant authorities, such as a financial or procurement authority.

Post-project review

The project manager is responsible for arranging a post-project review (PPR) that will take place shortly after the project is formally completed (end of transition phase). If the project is terminated early, the PPR will be then be conducted at the point of termination. The prime objective of the PPR is to learn lessons that may be appropriate to recommend improvements to other project management teams. A review document will be produced to describe the impact of approved changes on the project management plan and any benefits that can be assessed at this time, and to confirm that the quality of work done during the project meets the quality expectations of the customer and is most likely to be accepted.

All recommendations must be sufficiently robust for the organisation to be able to act upon them. Importantly, both project management and supporting business operations should be included in recommendations for incorporating in the organisation's guidelines for developing good practice for the planning and deployment of future projects.

Benefit review

A benefit (realisation) review is carried out during benefits realisation and is a formal review of a programme or project, typically conducted 6–12 months after handover and commissioning of the deliverables. These reviews may be repeated throughout the operational life of the product. This review is used to answer the question: 'Did we achieve what we set out to do, in business terms' and if not, what should be done?' For a construction, development or procurement project, a review is undertaken when there has been time to demonstrate the business benefits of a new service or building. For a major programme of change there will be several reviews over time. A benefits realisation review is an essential component of the benefits management process. It checks whether benefits, including those set out in the business case, have been achieved, and identifies opportunities for further improvement.

Audit

Normally undertaken by an independent body, which may be internal or external to the organisation but is independent from the project. An audit's objective is to provide assurance to the sponsor that the project is being managed using the agreed governance and process. Audits can be undertaken by a project management office, should one exist, and they form the foundation of assurance, providing confidence to stakeholders that projects will achieve their objectives and realise their benefits.

Think about...

the organisation that you work for or one that you have researched. Write down five aspects of a product or service produced by that organisation and how quality would be measured in these aspects to ensure customer acceptance.

2.2.5 Scope management

Learning objectives

This section considers how the translation of requirements into outputs for the chosen solution is achieved. There are a number of structures used that act as communication devices that allow a common perspective on the project to be gained by all interested stakeholders.

By the time you have studied this section you will have completed the following:

Learning outcome	Assessment criteria
5 Understand project scope management	**5.1** Define the term 'scope management'
	5.2 Differentiate between scope management within linear projects and scope management within iterative projects
	5.3 Describe how product breakdown structures (PBS) and work breakdown structures (WBS) are used to illustrate the required scope of work
	5.4 Outline how a project manager would use cost breakdown structures (CBS), organisational breakdown structures (OBS) and the responsibility assignment matrix (RAM)
	5.5 Define the terms 'configuration management' and 'change control' in the context of scope management
	5.6 Explain the relationship between change control and configuration management
	5.7 Outline the stages in a typical change control process
	5.8 Outline the activities in a typical configuration management process (including planning, identification, control, status accounting and verification audit)

The term 'scope management'

'Scope' is the term used in the management of projects to refer to the totality of the outputs, outcomes and benefits, and the work required to produce them. Outputs (deliverables) are the tangible or intangible products typically delivered by a project. Outcomes are the changed circumstances or behaviour that results from the use of an output and leads to realisation of benefits. Scope management is the process whereby outputs, outcomes and benefits are identified, defined and controlled. A high-level scope is typically recorded in the business case in support of the chosen option and its investment appraisal.

Scope management within linear and iterative projects

In projects with a linear life cycle, the baseline scope of work is defined through a breakdown structure to define the activities that will be scheduled and resourced to meet all the requirements and benefits. Scope definition in linear life cycle projects is assumed to be fixed. The time, cost and quality necessary to meet that scope is established in the remainder of the project planning process.

In projects using an iterative life cycle, it is equally important to structure the scope of work and record the assumptions. The difference in this scenario is that the 'must-have' requirements are prioritised in user stories and these are translated into a target scope of work to be achieved within a fixed time window with defined resources. Subsequent iterations may alter the scope based on accumulated experience, acquired insights and emerging priorities.

Using product breakdown structures (PBS) and work breakdown structures (WBS) to illustrate the required scope of work

The detailed scope of work emerges from the decomposition of the chosen option to meet the sponsor's requirements. Once a solution has been identified that meets the requirements, the scope of the work can be illustrated using a product breakdown structure (PBS). Identifying both products and the work involved in building them is an iterative activity. Where uncertainty about the end products exists, provision must be made for revisiting the PBS and the resultant work breakdown structure (WBS) during the project life cycle. The PBS is a hierarchical structure where the main output of the project is placed at the top level. The next level down shows the components that make up the higher level. This process continues to the level of individual products. Each product will have defined acceptance criteria and quality control methods.

For example, if an organisation wanted to organise an international conference in order to market its products to new markets overseas, the initial PBS might look like the example shown in Figure 2.2.5.1. The PBS shows what will be delivered. There is no detail provided, as yet, about the actual work required to complete these deliverables.

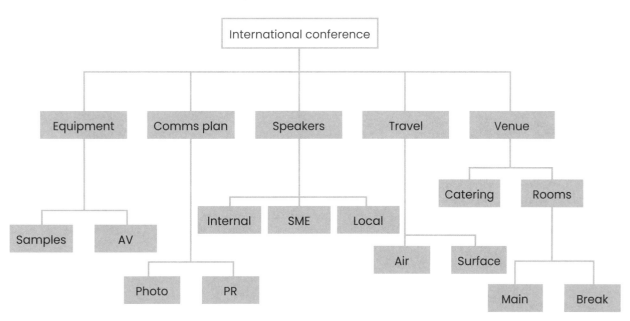

Figure 2.2.5.1 Example PBS for an international conference

Once the exercise of producing the PBS is complete, it can then be used to do initial scope verification to obtain stakeholders' agreement that the products identified are what they expect the project to deliver and get a firm agreement to that effect. At this stage it is hoped that stakeholders would also advise on what products are in or out of scope. Scope verification will continue, at various points, throughout the project until the deliverables have been finally handed over and formally accepted by stakeholders. Clearly defining what is in and out of scope prevents the risk of misunderstandings at a later point in the project, which may lead to emerging issues and change requests. Incomplete scope definition is a common cause of time delays, cost growth and benefit reduction.

Following the categorisation of the project to create products, the project manager is able to direct those products to the most suitable technical resource for more detailed scope definition. This results in the baseline scope of work to be defined through a WBS which will detail the activities that will be scheduled and resourced to meet all the requirements and benefits. The WBS derived from the example PBS shown in Figure 2.2.5.1 is shown in Figure 2.2.5.2.

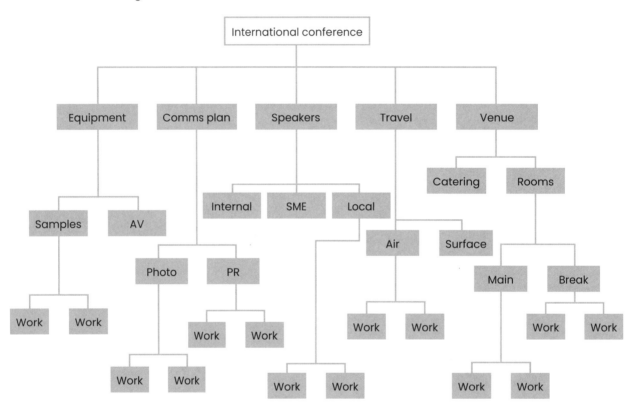

Figure 2.2.5.2 Example WBS structure derived directly from the PBS

At the lowest level of the WBS, work packages will exist that contain the activities to be performed to allow estimating, scheduling and resource assignments necessary to do the work and ultimately deliver the output. Where the objective is well understood and has a tangible output (e.g. in construction and engineering) it is usual to define the scope as accurately as possible at the beginning of the life cycle. Where the objective is less tangible, or subject to significant change, e.g. business change or some IT systems, a more flexible or iterative approach to scope is needed.

How a project manager would use cost breakdown structures (CBS), organisational breakdown structures (OBS) and the responsibility assignment matrix (RAM)

In the WBS each work package will have a coded reference in order to be tracked within the business management systems of the organisation. Any estimated costs related to the delivery of that work package, such as people, equipment, materials or any other resource required, can then be recorded using this coding structure. The resulting structure is the cost breakdown structure (CBS), a hierarchical breakdown of a project into cost elements. The CBS provides a financial view of the project and splits the project scope into its individual cost components, which can be related back to the original budget. The CBS will reflect the financial coding used for project accounting and any booking codes associated with each element of the project.

The work packages in the WBS are reviewed and decisions are made about who in the project will take responsibility for carrying out the work, supervising activity and reporting progress. The structure of the project organisation is vitally important for the effective performance of key activities and to support the efforts of the whole project team. The organisation breakdown structure (OBS) describes the structure of the project organisation required to complete the work packages in the WBS. This is particularly useful when work will be performed by business staff seconded to the project or by specialist teams working on more than one project. It is also important for individuals themselves to know where they are situated in the structure and their reporting responsibilities.

The WBS and OBS can be used in a combined way to create a communication device known as a responsibility assignment matrix (RAM). This ensures that the people who are going to do the work are fully aware of the work they have been assigned, together with their position in the project organisation. The functional line managers in the delivery organisation would also consult the RAM to confirm the work that has been assigned to their people. There are resource management systems that can allow the functional manager to approve assignments depending on individual availability and departmental workload. A common coding structure can be applied to the RAM as shown in Figure 2.2.5.3.

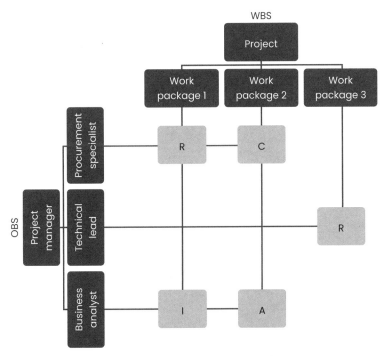

Figure 2.2.5.3 Responsibility assignment matrix (RAM) showing RACI coding

When the RAM is coded in this way it can also be referred to as a RACI matrix:

(R) Responsible – conducts the actual work/owns the problem

(A) Accountable – approves the completed work and is held fully accountable for it

(C) Consulted – included in decision-making, primary supportive role

(I) Informed – kept informed of progress and results

The RAM provides a clear and concise summary of tasks or deliverables, the specific responsibilities defined within the project procedures, and the level of accountability or contribution expected from named roles or individuals within the project.

The terms 'configuration management' and 'change control' in the context of scope management

Configuration management encompasses the technical and administrative activities concerned with the creation, maintenance, controlled change and quality control of the scope of work. A configuration consists of the functional and physical characteristics of the final deliverable as defined in technical documents and achieved in the execution of project management plans.

Change control is the process through which all requests to change the approved baseline of a project, programme or portfolio are identified, evaluated and then approved, rejected or deferred.

The relationship between change control and configuration management

Configuration management is very closely aligned with change control. There are two main points in the change control process where configuration management will provide support. First, when a change is being assessed, those who are responsible for making the decision will depend on configuration management supplying the most current versions of the plans, documents or specifications necessary for assessment to take place. Status accounting will provide a record showing how each document has changed and the status of the current documentation being used. It will also show any interdependencies between configuration items, an important aspect when assessing any knock-on effects of change.

The second point of support will be when the decision has been taken to implement a change. Once a change has been approved, all related documentation must be updated to reflect the change. The configuration record relating to all affected items will be updated accordingly. If any new changes are now being requested, configuration management will make sure that it is the updated version of all documentation that is released for review. The status of all previous versions will now be shown as superseded. Working together, these two processes ensure that deliverables meet the required specification, any changes are beneficial changes and there is a complete audit trail for the development of each deliverable. Figure 2.2.5.4 shows the flow through and relationship between these two processes.

While the configuration is primarily concerned with the products of a project or programme, it should also be applied to key management documents. For example, documents such as the business case and project management plan should be subject to version control and audit to ensure that they are fit for purpose and all changes are recorded.

As work is completed, responsibility for maintaining deliverables passes to business-as-usual. The project or programme management team is responsible for ensuring that configuration management information is suitable for transfer to those who will be maintaining the products long after the project or programme has been closed.

Stages in a typical change control process

Change requests may arise as a result of issues that relate to the management of the work, or from external sources such as new stakeholder requirements, new regulations or changes in the context that result in the original plans being no longer viable.

Managing requests for change effectively is a proven success factor in project management, the alternative being a potential escalation of problems as changes are adopted without analysis of their impact on other parts of the solution or deliverables. It is of particular importance when the project is part of a larger programme or portfolio, because the consequential effects of unmanaged change may be far-reaching within the planned change environment and to business-as-usual activities.

Managing change requests in a controlled way enables the sponsor and other stakeholders to:

- understand the implications of variations on the forecast outcomes of the work
- influence the decision on how to respond in the context of their objectives and appetite for risk

Figure 2.2.5.4 outlines the steps in a typical change control process. In scenarios where change is implemented without formal authorisation, the project manager adopts a retrospective process, which is often seen as unnecessary bureaucracy; however, this is needed to enable realistic forecasts.

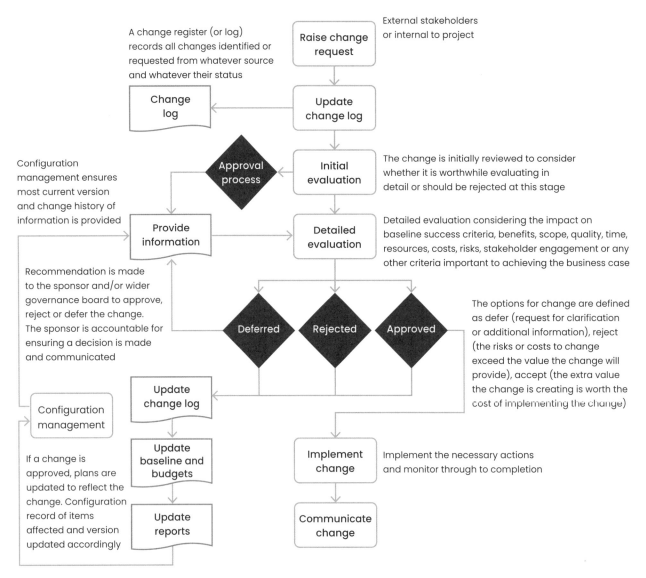

Figure 2.2.5.4 Stages in a typical change control process and relationship with configuration management

In certain circumstances, it is appropriate to implement a change freeze on a project where no further changes are considered, as failing to do so would jeopardise the achievement of the project objectives. In some industries, schedules of rates form the basis of pricing changes in advance of implementation. This eliminates the need to negotiate a price between contractor and client. Uncontrolled change in a contractual environment often leads to claims that may have to be settled in court.

Agile projects make change control an integral part of the development process. Each development iteration starts with a planning meeting that clarifies and prioritises the function addressed in the iteration. Some of these features may be changes to existing features, but these will still be considered alongside all the others.

Activities in a typical configuration management process

At its simplest, configuration management involves version control of documents and information, but the discipline of configuration management is a more complex endeavour in projects where the design of the solution is multifaceted, combining multiple technical disciplines and a wide range of asset types. The PBS, along with detailed descriptions of each product, becomes the project configuration. Once this is baselined it is subject to formal change control and configuration management.

The configuration management process shown in Figure 2.2.5.5 encompasses the following five activities:

Configuration management planning – A configuration management plan describes any project-specific procedures and the extent of their application. The plan also identifies roles and responsibilities for carrying out configuration management. The configuration management plan will often form part of the quality management plan but may be separate in large or complex projects.

Configuration identification – This involves breaking down the project into configuration items, and creating a unique numbering or referencing system for each type of item. For each item a configuration record is created that will record the current version and subsequent changes to the item.

Configuration control – Ensures that all changes to configuration items are controlled. As the previous step makes clear it is important to identify the interrelationships between configuration items to enable this.

Configuration status accounting – Provides records and reports that relate to a deliverable and its configuration information. It enables traceability of configuration items throughout their development. Users can consult the configuration record, which will provide an updated account of the status of the item, showing all changes to the current reference point, when these changes were made and who has taken responsibility for creating the latest version.

Configuration verification audit – This is used to determine whether a deliverable conforms to its requirements and configuration information. At a minimum, a verification audit is undertaken at the end of a life cycle phase, when a deliverable is finished or at the point of transitioning the output into use. However, audits could be carried out throughout the life cycle during change control to ensure management products are being used in line with their current configuration status.

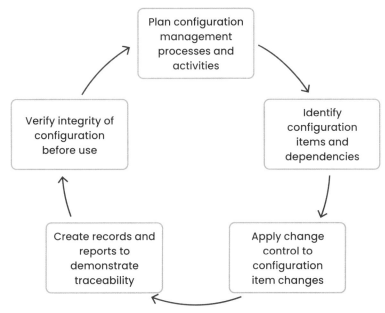

Figure 2.2.5.5 Activities involved in configuration management of an output

The key output of a well-controlled configuration management process is confidence that:

- the current version of any configuration item is known, be that a document, drawing, software or any other asset
- documented traceability exists between versions of each configuration item

Think about...

a project that you are familiar with or one that you have researched and write down five ways in which the customers requirements were established and controlled. How does this differ from the practices described in this section?

2.3 Achieving results

The results achieved will be proportional to the amount of upfront work, described in this section and the previous section. Success involves controlling deployment and ensuring that there is good information about progress and performance. This informs correct action and decision-making to ensure that the business case is delivered as well as possible. It is also about rigour in the areas studied up to this point – such as issue management, change control, configuration management and quality control – to ensure that good work put into early life cycle planning is not squandered by a lack of attention to detail in implementation.

Controlling deployment requires a detailed focus on monitoring and reporting as well as a commitment to manage risk, issues and change/variations in a disciplined way. The imperative to provide audit trails for assurance, and the opportunity for individual team members and the wider organisations involved to reflect, learn and improve, is an organisational reality for all who work in a competitive environment.

In the final analysis, people deliver projects and strong relationships with people underpin the administrative and bureaucratic disciplines required during deployment. Ultimately, engaging and influencing stakeholders, forming, building and leading teams, and the generic skills and responsibilities of being a project professional are addressed with the objective of making it clear that all project-based work relies fundamentally on the ability of people to work together.

Groups of people with a common aim are called a 'team' on the assumption that the people will not only cooperate with each other but also collaborate to innovate and perform. Effective project-based working relies on effective teamwork, often carried out in a context where teams are temporary, multidisciplinary and, occasionally, also geographically dispersed. Leading a group of people so they can become a high-performing team is skilled work and some would argue that it is the most important skill that a project professional needs to develop.

This final section of your learning journey includes:

2.3.1 Estimating

2.3.2 Resource scheduling and optimisation

2.3.3 Information management and reporting

2.3.4 Leadership and teamwork

2.3.1 Estimating

Learning objectives

This section considers how, once the scope of work has been defined, a prediction of time and resources required to complete that scope will need to be established.

By the time you have studied this section you will have completed the following:

Learning outcome	Assessment criteria
4 Understand project management planning	**4.8** State typical estimating methods (including analytical, analogous, parametric)
	4.9 Outline the purpose of the estimating funnel

Typical estimating methods

There is a choice of methods to produce an estimate. The actual method adopted will depend on the point in the life cycle where the estimate is being carried out, the time available and the amount of detailed information that exists concerning scope and working approaches.

Analytical

When the detailed scope of the project has been defined, usually through the formation of a work breakdown structure (WBS), detailed estimates can be produced for labour and non-labour resources to complete the activities in scope. This is often referred to as a bottom-up method, in that the task of producing the estimates will be delegated to those who are actually going to deliver the individual pieces of work or work packages. Their individual estimates are then summed from the bottom of the WBS to the top. For this estimating method to be valid, the WBS needs to be representative of the work that will eventually be carried out and so a verified WBS is essential to the accuracy of the final estimate. Analytical estimating can only be used to produce a cost estimate and not an estimate of duration. Summing the estimated durations from the bottom of the WBS to the top would not take account of work packages that will be conducted at the same time as others.

Analogous

This method is dependent on data being available about a similar project to the one being estimated. If the historical project was of the same size and similar complexity, and the method by which the new project is being delivered will be the same, then it is accepted that the cost of the previous project becomes the new estimate. It is possible to factor this estimate to take account of known variables, for example, by adding 10% to cover the known increases in material costs. When this estimate is produced at the start of the concept phase, it is often referred to as an order-of-magnitude estimate. To carry out this type of estimate the data on previous projects needs to be readily available. It is common that this estimate will provide the basis for the decision to proceed with the project.

Parametric

This estimating method uses a statistical relationship between historical data and other variables to calculate an estimate. The specifications of each deliverable are established together with the particular parameters that apply, for example, length of pipe, square footage of floor space or height of wall. Applied to these parameters are unit rates that are gained through either experience of doing the work previously or using rates that are produced by technical publishers as price books or books of norms. Parametric estimating can be one of the most accurate techniques for determining a project's duration and cost, provided the scope being estimated accurately represents the expected final requirements. When applying published data, care is required to ensure that the actual conditions of the work being estimated are similar to the conditions that have created the norms, and to take account of skill levels, lost-time factors and any physical aspects such as inclement weather.

The purpose of the estimating funnel

As the project progresses, project uncertainty will decline and, as a result, a different estimating method can be applied to verify previous estimates. This increase in accuracy from concept through to implementation is often termed the 'estimating funnel'. Note that as accuracy increases the level of contingency should decrease.

In the example shown in Figure 2.3.1.1, analogous estimates are first applied based on information available about prior projects. Whatever the source of the data, at this point in the life cycle the estimates produced have relatively broad ranges. During definition it is likely that a WBS is available and as verification takes place the duration/work estimating can be carried out for individual assignments. Using work packages improves the estimate accuracy and team member commitment. The overall estimate range has now reduced. During deployment the level of detail at this phase will allow parametric estimating, using either published rates or historical data from the organisation's own experience.

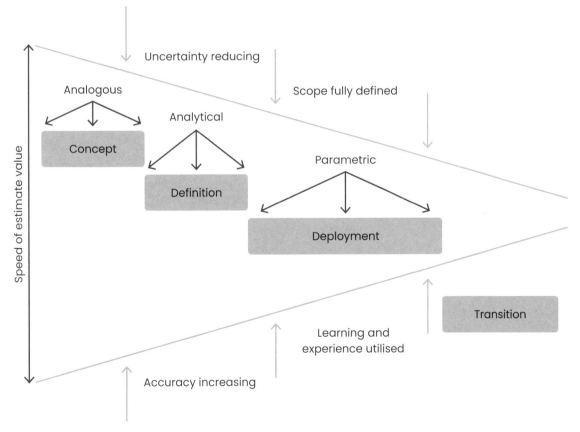

Figure 2.3.1.1 Estimating funnel showing factors that will influence the accuracy of the estimate

Think about...

a destination in the world that you would like to visit within the next year. While planning this visit you would like to produce an estimate of the travel time required. Write down at least five considerations that might affect the accuracy of your estimate of travel time.

2.3.2 Resource scheduling and optimisation

Learning objectives

This section considers the time schedule and considers techniques used to develop and present schedules that show when work within a project is planned to be performed. A project schedule can reside within a programme or portfolio schedule and have dependencies on the completion of other projects.

By the time you have studied this section you will have completed the following:

Learning outcome	Assessment criteria
6 Understand resource scheduling and optimisation in a project	**6.1** State the purpose of scheduling
	6.2 State the purpose of critical path analysis
	6.3 State the purpose of milestones
	6.4 Define the term 'timeboxing'
	6.5 Outline options for resource optimisation (including resource levelling and resource smoothing)
	6.6 Define the term 'procurement strategy'

The purpose of scheduling

A schedule is a timetable showing the forecast duration and the start and finish dates for activities or events within a project. Start and finish dates can be calculated with regard to available resources and external constraints as well as project logic. Once established, the schedule will be used throughout the project to:

- update progress, forecast performance and communicate this information to stakeholders
- show team members when tasks are due to be completed and the overall project duration
- show key milestones and progress towards achievement of these when work starts

Within a large project, there can be a number of individual schedules to deal with different aspects of the project. The master schedule combines, coordinates and keeps track of all subordinate schedules within the overall project scope.

The purpose of critical path analysis

Critical path analysis uses a scheduling technique to predict project duration by analysing which sequence of activities has the least amount of scheduling flexibility and is, therefore, critical if the planned overall duration is to be achieved. The critical path shows the sequence of these activities through a precedence network from start to finish, the sum of whose durations determines the overall duration.

Prior to any analysis being conducted, a project network is created from the agreed work packages and activities defined in the work breakdown structure, as shown in Figure 2.3.2.1. The dependencies exist because of the logical relationship between the activities dictated by the technical characteristics of each activity. In simple terms, the kettle can't be boiled until it is filled with water. Boiling the kettle is dependent on it being filled with water. Filling is a predecessor of boiling. The logical relationships between these two activities have now been established. Those who have the technical expertise and may also be delivering the work will collaborate to agree what the logical sequence of activities should be, ensuring that this is optimised as much as possible to be the most efficient way of delivering all the activities.

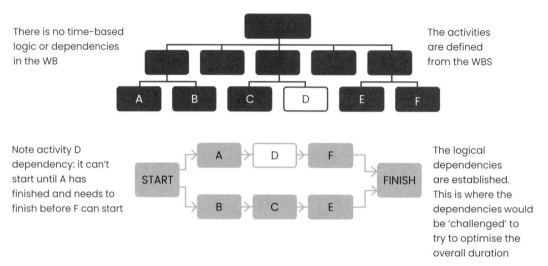

There is no time-based logic or dependencies in the WB

The activities are defined from the WBS

Note activity D dependency: it can't start until A has finished and needs to finish before F can start

The logical dependencies are established. This is where the dependencies would be 'challenged' to try to optimise the overall duration

Figure 2.3.2.1 Network created from work breakdown structure

Establishing the logic between the activities enables a precedence network to be determined that shows the relationship between activities. There are some common dependencies that are used when creating networks as shown in Figure 2.3.2.2.

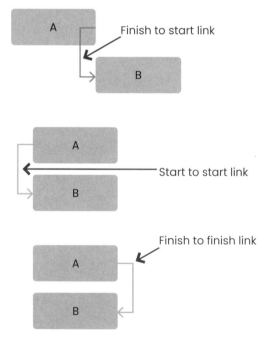

Figure 2.3.2.2 Common dependency types

The most common dependency is finish to start, and this acts as a default choice until sufficient information is known about the individual activities to consider an alternative.

Once the network has been created, then estimates of duration (based on the effort required) can be made. The resulting critical path can be identified as the longest pathway of activity, as seen in Figure 2.3.2.3.

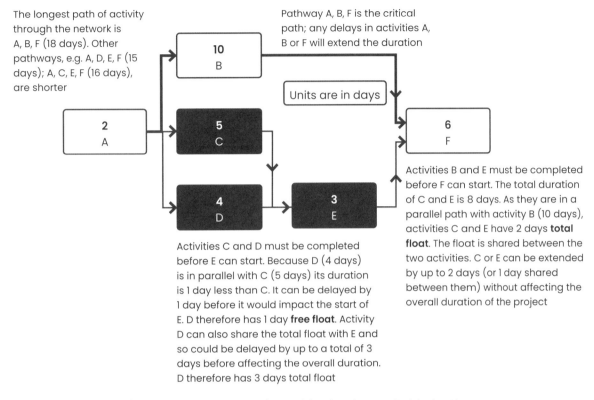

The longest path of activity through the network is A, B, F (18 days). Other pathways, e.g. A, D, E, F (15 days); A, C, E, F (16 days), are shorter

Pathway A, B, F is the critical path; any delays in activities A, B or F will extend the duration

Units are in days

10
B

2
A

5
C

6
F

4
D

3
E

Activities B and E must be completed before F can start. The total duration of C and E is 8 days. As they are in a parallel path with activity B (10 days), activities C and E have 2 days **total float**. The float is shared between the two activities. C or E can be extended by up to 2 days (or 1 day shared between them) without affecting the overall duration of the project

Activities C and D must be completed before E can start. Because D (4 days) is in parallel with C (5 days) its duration is 1 day less than C. It can be delayed by 1 day before it would impact the start of E. D therefore has 1 day **free float**. Activity D can also share the total float with E and so could be delayed by up to a total of 3 days before affecting the overall duration. D therefore has 3 days total float

Figure 2.3.2.3 Network showing activity durations and critical path

Figure 2.3.2.3 shows the critical path as activities A, B, F. Other pathways are shorter in their duration and are said to have float. The critical path also represents the shortest time to complete all activities in the logical order required.

'Float' is a term used to describe the flexibility with which an activity may be rescheduled. Float is created when a shorter-duration activity is in parallel with a longer-duration activity in the network. For example, if a 10-day activity was in parallel with an 8-day activity in the network, the 8-day activity would have 2 days float. This means that it could be moved, extended, delayed or split by up to 2 days without affecting the overall duration of the project. It is useful to identify float and it is mainly used to help schedule activities within resource constraints. There are various types of float, such as total float and free float.

Total float is defined as the time by which an activity may be delayed or extended without affecting the overall duration or violating a target finish date. Free float is defined as the time by which an activity may be delayed or extended without affecting the start of any succeeding activity.

The purpose of milestones

A milestone is defined as a key event selected for its importance in the schedule, commonly associated with tangible acceptance of deliverables. It is good practice to produce a milestone schedule to show stakeholders the major milestones and for reporting current and forecast progress.

Once the network analysis has been completed and the network optimised a Gantt chart is created to show the activities against a timeline (see Figure 2.3.2.4). Milestones are entered into the schedule as if they were an activity, but they have zero duration and therefore act as markers, rather than having any duration in the timeline. In this simple example, the milestones are shown as black diamond shapes and so they are easy to see within the detail of the bar chart. However, if this was a more complex schedule with many more activities, the milestones may not be as visible.

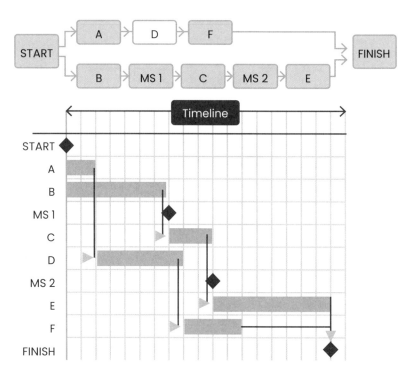

Figure 2.3.2.4 Network and Gantt chart showing milestones

There are a number of stakeholders, such as the sponsor or senior management, who do not need to know the detail of specific tasks, floats and dependencies, etc. They do, however, need a high-level summary of current progress. A milestone chart will provide the necessary level of communication.

The milestone chart will show a stripped-down version of the schedule with activity bars removed, as shown in Figure 2.3.2.5. This example (timeline in weeks) shows the project milestones at a reference time, 'Time now'. From this chart it can be seen that the project has started on time; however, it is forecast that milestone MS 1 is to be achieved two weeks later than planned. The delay in reaching MS 1 seems to be causing a forecast delay on MS 2 of four weeks and a delay of the finish milestone of three weeks. Hopefully the early warning created by the forecast will prompt action to be taken that might reduce the slippage.

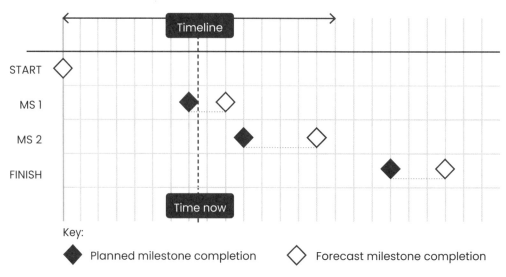

Figure 2.3.2.5 Milestone chart

The term 'timeboxing'

Many agile methods apply the idea of timeboxing, where an iterative life cycle is adopted that seeks to deliver value in an incremental way, rather than adopting a linear (or waterfall) life cycle, which aims to deliver value at the end of the project. A timebox is an iteration with a fixed end date that is not allowed to change, thereby adjusting the scope and quality to deliver on time and to cost. The agile approach will commit to delivering on time and so each iteration may have several timeboxes. Multiple timebox iterations are likely to be employed in parallel to develop different aspects of the deliverable. Having such a rigid approach to time planning maintains the team's focus on achieving targeted goals. Overall, using iterations allows earlier return on some of the benefits that have already been implemented while validating the concepts and engaging users.

Options for resource optimisation (including resource levelling and resource smoothing)

The main objective of resource optimisation is to make sure that all resources are used optimally. There are several stages to building up a clear picture of how the resources will be used to deliver the required scope. The first stage is to allocate suitable resources to each of the tasks. Checks will ensure that they have the right skills and competencies to do the assigned work. Once resource allocation is complete, the resource demand profile can be viewed using a resource histogram, a block graph showing the quantity of resource that has been allocated over the time schedule, as shown in Figure 2.3.2.6.

Resources are allocated to each activity. In this example the resources per unit of time, required to do the work as scheduled, are: A1, B2, C1, D2, E2 and F3

The resource requirements can be graphed in a resource histogram to show the demand profile

The resource histogram demand profile will be reviewed against current maximum resource availability (4 in this example)

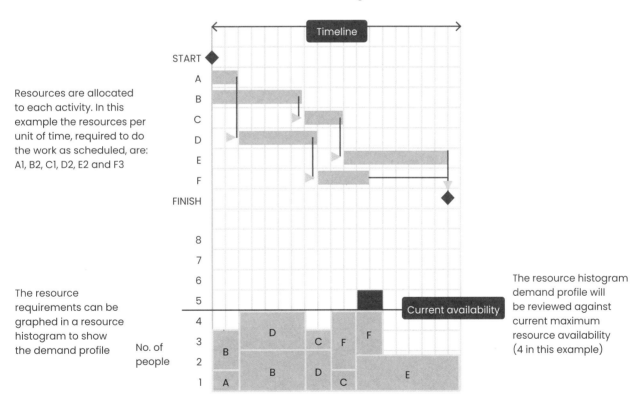

Figure 2.3.2.6 Resource histogram showing the demand profile resulting from resource allocation decisions

Figure 2.3.2.6 shows that the work can't be done as scheduled as the current availability of resource is limited to four and the allocation to activity F exceeds that limit.

There are two basic options available to the project manager: resource levelling and resource smoothing.

Resource levelling (resource-limited scheduling) answers the question: With the resources available, when will the work be finished? Levelling is used where resource availability is limited, for example, specialists or complex testing equipment, or where there might be space or accommodation restrictions.

Resource levelling can be achieved in the project by:

- Redefining the scope of the activities to be undertaken by the particular resource concerned. In simple terms, this might mean giving some of the work to an under-utilised resource.
- Redefining the specification (avoiding, if possible, any compromise to the quality of the final product).
- Increasing task duration to reduce the overall resource requirements.
- Increasing resources on earlier tasks to bring workload forward, such that peaks in the future are reduced. This will have cost, and possibly quality, implications.
- Moving activities that are not on the critical path to reduce demand at peak times – i.e. using free and total float to optimise the schedule.

Figure 2.3.2.7 shows the result of resource levelling, where activity F has been extended by removing one resource and spreading the activity over an additional two time periods. The activity has been extended within its available float, so will not have any effect on the overall duration. For this to be possible in practice, it assumes that the activity will behave in the desired manner. It may not be realistic to think that an activity duration will expand or contract in exact proportion to the people being added or removed. Prior to making effective resource optimisation decisions a thorough examination of the task and its technical characteristics would be necessary.

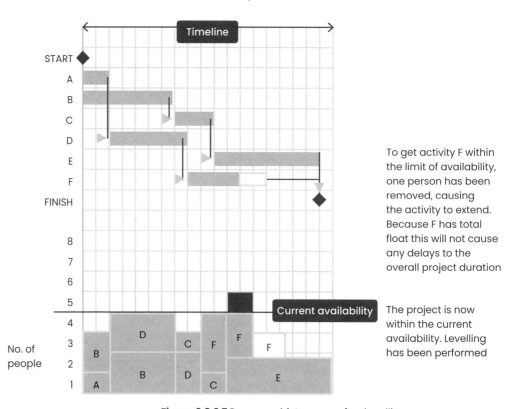

To get activity F within the limit of availability, one person has been removed, causing the activity to extend. Because F has total float this will not cause any delays to the overall project duration

The project is now within the current availability. Levelling has been performed

Figure 2.3.2.7 Resource histogram after levelling

When all levelling options have been considered and a solution is still unavailable, the project duration will extend but hopefully this will be minimised as much as possible.

Resource smoothing (time-limited scheduling) is used when time is more important than cost. The objective is to deliver the work within the fixed timescale. This may involve reducing the duration of activities by adding resources, for example, more people, the same number of people working longer hours, or additional equipment, and then trying to get a 'smooth' usage of resources, avoiding peaks and troughs of resource demand and optimising the flow of resources from one piece of work to another.

Resource smoothing needs to be considered on a resource-by-resource basis, particularly when a reduction in the overall duration of the schedule is required, perhaps in response to changing time priorities. Applying additional resources to critical-path activities is the only way the overall schedule will be impacted. If additional resources were to be applied to activities with float, it would just provide additional float to those activities, with no impact on the duration overall. Resource smoothing will ensure that any peaks and troughs will be smoothed out when additional resources are being applied.

Achieving a smoothed resource profile may require some redefinition of the order of some of the work, where the logic used originally was discretionary, not mandatory, for example, where work could be done in parallel rather than in sequence. Achieving the optimally resourced schedule can be a creative process requiring multiple iterations to get the best result possible.

There is, of course, a finite limit to the resource that can be put into some tasks due to the nature of the task and the environment. For example, a task involving data entry will be impacted very little by additional resource if there is only one data terminal available. If resource really is finite, there are no more hours available from skilled people or no more equipment is available, then there is no option but to extend durations and the overall project time to accommodate this, as shown in Figure 2.3.2.8.

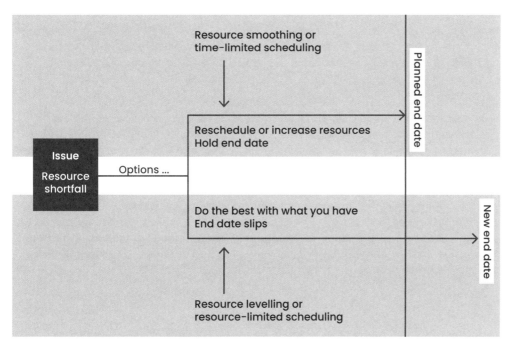

Figure 2.3.2.8 Resource levelling and smoothing options

The term 'procurement strategy'

The procurement strategy is the high-level approach for securing the goods and services required from external suppliers to satisfy project, programme and portfolio needs. External suppliers will often be contractor organisations, but may also be another department or division of the host organisation. Where the external source is a separate legal entity, the terms under which goods and services are procured will be the subject of a legal contract, which will outline the legally binding obligations between the various parties. When the supply source is part of the same organisation, an internal service-level agreement may be used.

Decisions to make with the sponsor and wider governance are:

- How much risk to retain in the project and how much to share with suppliers in the supply chain?
- On a continuum from transactional (based solely on price and supply) to collaborative (considering a more integrated relationship and working together to serve parties' interests), what type of relationship is desired with different suppliers, and why?

The complexity of the work, the capability of the team, the client/owner's appetite for risk and the analysis of the market are all considered prior to deciding what procurement route is best. The resulting procurement strategy for the project considers:

- make or buy decision – do the work in-house or procure external contractor
- supplier selection – objective selection following required process
- contractual relationship – type of contract for required work with suitable terms and conditions
- reimbursement methods – on what basis will suppliers be paid: fixed sum, variable, milestone payment
- contract administration – managing service delivery and ensuring contractual performance

Stand-alone projects may be able to take advantage of procurement arrangements set up by the host organisation. Similarly, those that are part of a programme may find that much of the procurement is handled at the higher level. Delivery contractors often have to use their client's procurement process and choice of supplier as part of the conditions of contract.

When a project has specialist, or unique, requirements it will need access to procurement specialists and must consider procurement implications as early in the life cycle as is practicable. Waiting until the full approval of the project at the end of the definition phase may, for example, result in tender delays and long lead times having a detrimental effect on the schedule.

In some projects, procured resources can represent the majority of the cost, so a rigorous procurement process is vital to success. It is common for organisations to hold approved supplier listings and carry out periodic audits to provide assurance of quality, capability and capacity to deliver. All procurement involves risk and all aspects of the resource management plan must be prepared with risk management in mind.

2.3.3 Information management and reporting

Learning objectives

This section considers the processes for managing project data that is essential for effective delivery of the project. All project stakeholders rely on accurate and timely information for teams and stakeholders to make informed decisions and fulfil their role in a cost-efficient and effective way.

By the time you have studied this section you will have completed the following:

Learning outcome	Assessment criteria
4 Understand project management planning	**4.11** Outline the purpose and benefits of project progress reporting

Information management is the process that includes the collection, storage, curation, dissemination, archiving and destruction of documents, images, drawings and other sources of information. Project documentation should be considered a reliable information source to communicate to all stakeholders and to provide documentary evidence for assurance.

Many organisations have standard forms and tools to manage information, potentially supported by a project management office (PMO). Computer software packages exist to manage such tasks, optimising the use of existing data and allowing it to be harvested to build project analytics, which is vital for the organisation to develop its project management maturity and learning. Standard templates are useful to help with assurance and process improvement. These are documented in the information management plan, a section of the project management plan, and approved by governance.

Information management works closely with the communication management processes. The communication plan identifies the stakeholders that will require some form of communication about the project and its progress. Information management identifies the type of information that will be sent to those stakeholders and the timing of that information. Not all stakeholders should receive reports concerning all aspects of the project, but those stakeholders who are required to make decisions about the project must receive their information in a timely manner.

Purpose and benefits of project progress reporting

The purpose of project progress reporting is to ensure the provision of accurate and timely information for teams and stakeholders to keep track of deliverables and make informed decisions to fulfil their role in a cost-efficient and effective way. There are three elements required for any performance measurement: a baseline to measure against; data on actual performance; and an assessment of the implications of the performance to date. Progress monitoring enables meaningful reports to be presented to the sponsor and governance board to enable appropriate decisions to be made to improve performance.

There are several pieces of information that will typically be reported on throughout the project and the project manager will use this information in a number of ways to help ensure successful project outcomes:

- **Performance status** – Actual or forecast date of achievement for the deliverables.
- **Schedule status** – Estimated time of completion for each task.
- **Cost status** – Actual expenditure and the committed expenditure to date for each task.
- **Status of quality progress** – Changes that might affect the form or function of the task deliverables.
- **Risk exposure system** – Changes in the status of any identified threats to the achievement of tasks, together with any new threats or opportunities.
- **Exception thresholds and variance reporting** – Defined triggers will require the task owner to report variations to forecast time and cost at completion, and suggest recovery actions.
- **Motivation and satisfaction of team members.**
- **Performance of contractors and the health of the relationships in the supply chain.**
- **Effectiveness of communication with stakeholders.**

The project manager will have several uses for this reported information. Schedule status information will be reviewed and the schedule updated. Any variances reported to the schedule for time and cost will be noted and, if necessary, corrective action will be taken to bring the tasks back onto the appropriate time and cost schedule. The project manager will use information as a basis for reporting to the sponsor and steering group and other stakeholders as indicated by the communications plan.

Information received from the task owners will be formed into a consolidated report. Information from the task owners and teams is received frequently, often weekly, while the consolidated report is required at a lower frequency, often monthly. The reporting of status may trigger an issue that will require escalating to the sponsor and/or steering group, sometimes referred to as exception reporting. It could also be used as a basis for performance reviews with the teams concerned, particularly with a view to continual improvement, for example, when reviewing the quality statistics.

Information from teams could also be used to support valuations of work performed and related payments. As there will be a significant amount of information analysis to be undertaken in a large project, the project manager may be assisted by the PMO in this task.

Think about...

a project you know or one you have researched. Write down five ways in which the project reports its progress to stakeholders.

2.3.4 Leadership and teamwork

Learning objectives

This section considers how leadership can enable people coming together from different functions, disciplines and organisations to work with a common purpose to deliver something of value to the investing organisation.

By the time you have studied this section you will have completed the following:

Learning outcome	Assessment criteria
10 Understand leadership and teamwork within a project	**10.1** Define the term 'leadership'
	10.2 Explain how a project team leader can influence team performance
	10.3 Outline the challenges to a project manager when developing and leading a project team
	10.4 Outline how a project manager can use models to assist team development (including Belbin and Tuckman)

The term 'leadership'

Leadership is described as the ability to establish vision and direction, to influence and align others towards a common purpose, and to empower and inspire people to achieve success. There are many theories of leadership and the subject can be approached in a variety of ways. One simple approach to understanding different leadership styles is the comparison of transactional leaders and transformational leaders.

Transactional leaders ensure that requirements are agreed and that the rewards and penalties for achievement, or lack of it, are understood. It is an exchange process to do with setting objectives and plans: 'do this and you will be rewarded thus'.

In contrast, transformational leaders do everything possible to help people succeed in their own right and become leaders themselves. They help those people to transform themselves and achieve more than was intended or even thought possible.

How a project team leader can influence team performance

By definition, the project environment is one of change. New teams come together to achieve objectives and are disbanded when the work is complete. As a consequence, the project manager should focus on different aspects of leadership throughout the project life cycle and set the pace accordingly.

Early phases may require expertise in influencing stakeholders and creating vision, and need a more transactional style with the project team. As the work progresses, the leadership focus shifts to maintaining momentum, responding to change and applying a more transformational approach.

The position of leader is granted by followers who make the decision to follow. That decision will be influenced by the leader using an appropriate style of leadership that takes account of both the situation and the readiness of people to follow. Team members' willingness to follow will vary according to their levels of motivation and ability, as well as their loyalties and priorities, and the context of the situation.

Challenges to a project manager when developing and leading a project team

Leadership is needed at all levels within a project-based setting. The sponsor communicates the vision to the project team, sets high-level expectations, involves team members in decisions and provides actionable feedback. The project manager should fully understand how to get the best out of each person, and should provide direction and support for them. Team members share responsibilities and work collaboratively. All leaders must provide timely and constructive feedback, and also be receptive to feedback provided to them by members of the team.

Leaders need to adapt their style and approach to the needs of the team and the work that needs to be accomplished; this is called Situational Leadership®. Figure 2.3.4.1 shows the factors that influence leadership styles and the varying styles that can be adopted in the Situational Leadership® model. There are some situations when the leader needs to be directive, for example, to address an issue that threatens the achievement of objectives.

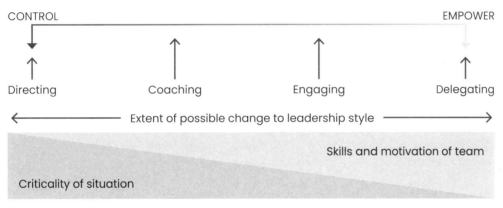

Figure 2.3.4.1 Factors that contribute to variance in leadership style

A mentoring or coaching style is appropriate when there is time to focus on development of the team as well as goal achievement. For much of the time, when the team is established and working well, the leader delegates responsibility for achieving activities to team members, only intervening if evidence arises to suggest that performance is not to agreed expectations. Leadership in a project context is usually performed with limits on the leader's power, requiring them to adopt a style that builds team and wider stakeholder commitment.

Situational Leadership® provides choices of leadership style. Is there a best choice? The answer is a qualified 'yes', providing that the leader takes account of two aspects. First, the criticality of the situation: the more critical the situation, the more the leader may have to exert control and adopt a directing style. Communication between leader and team is short, sharp and commanding. Second, the skills and motivation of the team members: the greater the team's abilities, the more the leader can empower the team to complete tasks, perhaps adopting a more delegating style.

The main challenge for a leader in considering a Situational Leadership® approach is having a good background knowledge of the individual team members' skill levels and some insight into their levels of motivation. In addition, they need to have a developed degree of situational awareness to make quick, reliable assessments of the nature of the situation and implications of any delays in response.

In general, teamwork has benefits to both the individual team members themselves and any organisation seeking to deliver multiple projects and programmes. Teamwork creates collaboration in the workplace, which can result in more flexible work schedules, particularly when team members are cross-trained to cover for each other's skills and strengths. It's also important to note that flexible working is increasingly being considered as a way to help improve productivity and develop a better work–life balance for employees.

Another challenge for the project manager is the responsibility for delivering the intended outputs and outcomes when they may have had little say about who joins the team and whether the chosen team members have the right skills and attributes.

This makes the ability of the project manager to develop and lead teams of vital importance. The simplest project has people who take on the roles of sponsor, project manager and team members – even if they are part-time roles as part of a wider job. Iterative and agile projects may involve small dedicated teams including a product owner or on-site customer.

As projects get larger, the project manager role is typically supported by specialists in aspects of project-based working, for example, schedulers, cost estimators, risk facilitators, communication specialists or business change leaders. Some team members may span multiple organisations, for example, suppliers, partners or customer/client staff as members of the deployment team. Additional skills to develop and lead the team across organisational and cultural boundaries are needed in this situation.

Some teams are co-located in the same geographic area. Where this is possible there are distinct benefits from the ability to share a physical space where plans and progress can be visualised, and close working relationships can be developed.

How a project manager can use models to assist team development

For teams to be effective it is important that team members are understood as individuals in terms of their capabilities, their preferences, their cultural norms and expectations, and the social dynamics between team members. By paying attention to team development, project managers can create positive working cultures that enable high performance of the team and an increased chance of success.

As soon as a team forms it is unlikely, at that stage, to achieve the performance levels that match the individual capabilities of the group members. Psychological researcher Bruce Tuckman observed that teams will typically go through different stages of maturity over time before reaching their optimum performance levels. The Tuckman model (Tuckman, 1977) identified five stages a team will progress through, from when the team is formed to when the team is disbanded.

An important aspect of this model is that the team does not pass through these stages naturally. Progress through each stage is facilitated by effective leadership actions. The team leader has a key role in helping the team move through these stages as efficiently as possible and re-addressing stages as new team members join or others leave. The Tuckman model is shown in action in Figure 2.3.4.2 and outlines the stages as:

Forming

This is the first point of contact that team members have in this project context. Their knowledge of the project or environmental circumstances is very limited. Team members are naturally guarded. At this stage the leader will ensure that they communicate clear goals and objectives, creating an inclusive and coordinated environment.

Storming

The team members now start to understand that they will be unable to achieve goals on their own and that cooperation is expected. It is at this stage where individual personalities start to influence how team members interact with each other. The biggest issue at this stage is conflict created through competition and disagreements about how to achieve project objectives. If conflict is not managed it can cause the team to reverse to forming, with team members closing down and communication being reduced. The leader has a strong role to ensure differences are aired and conflict is resolved in a positive way.

Norming

If conflict is resolved successfully the team members start to become much more cooperative with each other as they start to focus on the tasks required to achieve objectives. This stage is very much felt by the team as a need for balance; team cohesion is important but not to the detriment of getting the work done. The leadership priority at this stage is to provide processes, clear roles and responsibilities, and timely feedback.

Performing

The team is now delivering the targeted performance. Creative problem-solving and motivation are at their highest levels. The leader will ensure performance is maintained by promoting openness, honesty and the development of trusting relationships. Now that the team has experienced achievement it is likely that this will continue; however, it can't be taken for granted. The team could actually revert to one of the earlier stages, usually in response to change, for example, due to team members leaving and new people joining, or changing the scope of the tasks. The degree of reversal depends on the scale of the change but also on the strength of the leader. Strong leadership means that with even a large-scale change, the team may only revert to norming for a short time before returning to performing. The opposite is also true. For example, under weak leadership a small change can cause the team to completely collapse, returning to forming.

Adjourning

This was a stage that Tuckman identified several years after developing the original four-stage model. This stage acknowledges the efforts of the leader in preparing team members for the end of one team and the start of a new team in the future. Providing feedback on individual performance, liaising with functional management and recognising achievement are just some of the leadership tasks necessary at this stage, all with the aim of ensuring that team members are transitioned effectively back into the business or their organisation.

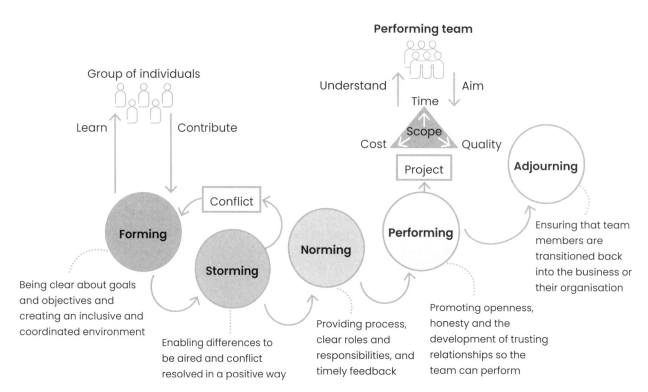

Figure 2.3.4.2 Stages of team development and leadership actions necessary to reach performance

The establishment of a team will initially involve the selection of individuals based on their skills, behaviours and attitudes. When people with complementary skills and behaviours are committed to a common objective and method of working it is likely that they will be able to reach performing within a reasonable time, even with moderate leadership. Another factor that has also been studied is the influence of different personalities working together and how they might have an effect on teamworking.

Cambridge psychologist Meredith Belbin produced a model to show how different personalities work together to create an effective team. Belbin described nine social roles (Belbin, 2010) that individuals adopt and the strengths and weaknesses of each. Within a team, one person's strengths balance another's weaknesses. Individuals will perform better in a team context if they are given a role that plays to their strengths. The nine team roles are equally grouped into three clusters, action, social and thinking, as shown in Figure 2.3.4.3.

Figure 2.3.4.3 Belbin's nine social roles
Source: www.Belbin.com

Action

The Shaper will provide the necessary drive to ensure that the team keeps moving and does not lose focus or momentum. The Implementer will plan a workable strategy and carry it out as efficiently as possible. Most effectively used at the end of tasks to polish and scrutinise the work for errors, the Completer Finisher will subject output to the highest standards of quality control.

Social

The Resource Investigator uses their inquisitive nature to find ideas to bring back to the team, and is excellent at communicating from the project to stakeholders. The Team Worker is the diplomat of the team, helping the team to gel, using their versatility to identify the work required and complete it on behalf of the team. The Coordinator's role is necessary to focus on the team's objectives, draw out team members and delegate work appropriately.

Thinking

When the team is faced with obstacles and needs to be highly creative and good at solving problems in unconventional ways, the Plant provides the necessary support to allow the team to function well in these circumstances. The Monitor Evaluator provides a logical eye, making impartial judgements where required, and weighs up the team's options in a dispassionate way. When the team requires in-depth knowledge in key areas, the Specialist is a member of the team who has distinct strengths in a very narrow area.

Think about...

a team you are a member of now or have been in the past. Write down five things that you think make it a good team and/or five things that could be improved to make the team function better. Consider also the role of the leader in facilitating team spirit.

Read about... The world of project management

Many of the traditional team assessment models assume that the team members will be working together and will have regular contact with each other. Current communication technology now allows teams to be apart from each other and still perform as a team. An article published in *Project* considered some of the challenges that surround virtual teams.

Dispersed teams

Virtual working, with team members dispersed around the world, presents a series of challenges of its own, the most obvious of which is time difference. Finding times when everyone can talk together can be particularly difficult. Forming emotional bonds between team members, and avoiding miscommunication, are other well-rehearsed issues for virtual teams.

"Even when webcams are used, there are misunderstandings because you are not seeing the non-verbal gestures people make," says Sean Dubberke, New York-based director of learning with training organisation RW3 CultureWizard. "And on electronic platforms, like email, chat or SMS, it's common for people to misunderstand what has been said."

Put the two things together – multiple cultures and virtual teamworking – and the challenges are augmented. Key areas include language, communication, relationship building and working styles.

Originally published in *Project* Winter 2019.

If you would like to read more about this example or other real-world project examples, copies of APM's *Project* journal can be downloaded from the members' resources area of the APM website: apm.org.uk/project.

Chapter 3

Self-assessment

3.1 Test questions

These short quizzes are designed to give you a quick insight into your knowledge of each section as you work through the guide and so will give you feedback on your progress. The questions are in the order of the main study text. Complete the questions in each section and choose one answer from the four choices given. Check your answers at the end of this section and refer back to the main text to revise your learning.

Section 2 – Short quiz

2.1 Introducing projects

2.1.1 Project environment

1 PESTLE analysis covers the following areas:

    A Political, Economic, Sociological, Technological, Legal, Environmental.

    B Personnel, Economic, Safety, Technological, Legal, Ecological.

    C Political, Ecological, Strategy, Technological, Life cycle, Environmental.

    D Personnel, Ecological, Sociological, Training, Life cycle, Ecological.

2 Which of the following best describes a project's context?

    A The environment in which the business operates.

    B The geographic location in which the project is undertaken.

    C The external and internal business environments including stakeholders' interests and influences.

    D Industry and business sector practices.

3 When managing the internal context, the project manager should especially be aware of:

    A organisational strategy, policies and frameworks.

    B competitive positioning.

    C new legislation.

    D business continuity.

4 To be fully effective, the project manager:

A must take into consideration the internal and external environments.

B need only deal with the internal environment since the sponsor will deal with the external environment.

C should manage the external stakeholders and external environment.

D must liaise with regulating bodies to ensure requirements include the latest legislation.

5 Which type of project needs to consider environmental constraints?

A Construction projects only.

B Construction and petrochemical projects only.

C All but IT projects.

D All projects.

6 What is the best way that PESTLE analysis supports the development of a business case?

A It provides a powerful way in which the most favourable financial returns are shown from the project options being considered.

B It considers a number of options, avoiding over-reliance on a single idea, when there may be other more favourable options available.

C It identifies which tools and techniques are necessary in order to arrive at the best group of projects to be considered as valid options.

D It shows which assets, capabilities, processes and functions are required to be included in the business case.

7 When using a PESTLE analysis, a potential change in national government would be an example of a:

A a political factor.

B an economic factor.

C a sociological factor.

D a potential change of government would not be considered in such an analysis.

8 Which of the following aspects would best describe part of the project environment?

A The influence and interests of the key stakeholders of the project.

B The technical difficulties that are anticipated when undertaking the project.

C The circumstances within which the project is being undertaken.

D The relationship between the project manager and the project team.

9 What would be a most likely result for an organisation following a PESTLE analysis?

A The organisation would know what political change is most likely and therefore the impacts on objectives considered.

B The organisation would most likely have a number of options available as to how the desired objectives could be achieved.

C The organisation would have an understanding of the necessary skills required to deliver the objectives required.

D The organisation would be able to develop an accurate estimate of the costs and time frame for the objectives to be achieved.

10 Which of the following is true of the project environment?

   A Within the environment are the factors that influence and impact projects.

   B Only certain types of projects are influenced by the environment.

   C The project environment will only really impact the project at the start.

   D There is no real way of determining the true project environment.

11 Why is environmental analysis the most important analysis for an organisation to undertake?

   A It allows the definition of the detailed execution plans that are likely to be developed in order to deliver the project.

   B It is the only way in which the scope of the project can be identified and detailed in plans.

   C It identifies the problems, opportunities or business needs which may require some degree of response.

   D It is the only form of detailed planning that can be carried out in the earliest phases of the project life cycle.

12 What is the most likely conclusion resulting from a PESTLE analysis?

   A The agreed end date for the project.

   B A list of possible stakeholders.

   C The number of project phases necessary.

   D The size of the project team required.

NOW CHECK YOUR ANSWERS AT THE END OF THIS SECTION. YOUR SCORE: /12

2.1.2 Project, programme and portfolio management

1 Which of the following is a characteristic of a project rather than business-as-usual?

    A Sustain the organisation to achieve its business purpose and goals.

    B Repetitive, non-unique product, service or result.

    C Formal line authority over functional unit personnel.

    D Achieve objectives, then terminate.

2 Which one of the following is a consideration of project management?

    A Making sure that operational management objectives are maintained as projects are delivered.

    B Planning and executing effective communications within the project.

    C Measuring business benefits of projects to ensure that, in retrospect, they have been a worthwhile consideration.

    D Setting the organisation's standards for excellence in project delivery.

3 Which of the following illustrates why project management is the most efficient way of managing change?

    A It provides recommendations for the organisation to follow for employing a consultancy firm that specialises in change management.

    B It provides a profile of the skills required when employing project managers.

    C It ensures that the head of the organisation will always be accountable for achieving the benefits of all projects undertaken by that organisation.

    D It utilises resources as and when required under the direction of a manager with single-point responsibility.

4 Which of the following is not a characteristic of business-as-usual?

    A Recruitment of new project managers.

    B Operating new production machinery.

    C Training of operations staff to become more safety-aware.

    D Introducing change.

5 When delivering a project, the project manager has to balance which of the following constraints?

    A Configuration and delivery.

    B Time, cost and quality.

    C Cost, scope and change.

    D Budget, cost and risk.

6 Which of these is not a project management activity?

    A Recruitment of project managers.

    B Producing a business case.

    C Carrying out a post-project review.

    D Benefits realisation.

7 Which of the following would be considered the best description of a project?

    A A group of activities that are required to deliver a portion of work.

    B A method of planning how work should be conducted.

    C A sum of activities needed to meet specific objectives.

    D A set of techniques used to deliver change.

8 Which one of the following would be most suited to a project management approach?

    A Maintaining existing systems.

    B Operating new systems.

    C Minor changes to existing systems.

    D Introducing new systems.

9 Throughout the life of the project, schedule, cost and performance are always considered to be:

    A fixed throughout the life of the project.

    B at the discretion of the project manager.

    C agreed between project manager and business sponsor.

    D the same for all projects regardless of outcome.

10 Teams formed within an organisational structure and aligned to suit functional demands would best describe:

    A business-as-usual.

    B a project.

    C a programme.

    D a portfolio.

11 Which one of the following examples would most likely be delivered using a project management approach?

    A Designing and building a prototype for a new type of electric vehicle.

    B Managing the delivery of goods and services within a fixed-term contract.

    C A drilling rig drilling multiple wells in a three-year exploration of new oil fields.

    D Managing the first human space trip to explore the surface of Mars.

12 Programme management could be defined as?

    A The coordinated line management of a team of programme and project managers to achieve beneficial change.

    B The coordinated management of a functional area of the business serving a number of different projects and programmes.

    C The coordinated management of progress concerning a programme of activities identified in the project schedule.

    D The coordinated management of projects and business-as-usual activities to achieve beneficial change.

13 One of the key benefits of programme management is that:

    A it enables every project to be covered by one all-embracing plan.

    B it reduces the need to assign priorities to individual projects within the programme.

    C dependencies and interfaces between projects can be managed to greater business advantage.

    D management time can be saved by grouping projects together under a single distinct programme.

14 Which of the following is a key part of programme management?

    A Benefits management.

    B Quality management.

    C Scope management.

    D Operations management.

15 One responsibility of the programme manager is to:

    A coordinate the planners between projects.

    B manage dependencies and interfaces between projects.

    C ensure delivery to time according to the project schedule.

    D manage interfaces between teams on a project.

16 Which is the correct statement? The programme manager can be responsible for:

    A managing resource priorities between projects.

    B carrying out post-project reviews.

    C defining the project responsibility assignment matrix.

    D undertaking configuration management.

17 In most circumstances, which of the following could not be specifically attributed as a benefit of programme management?

    A More efficient use of resources.

    B Improved teamworking.

    C More effective delivery of benefits.

    D Project objectives linked to strategic objectives.

18 Portfolio management could be defined as:

    A a group of projects brought together to form a strategic programme.

    B the development of expertise and competency throughout the whole organisation.

    C the strategic business plan that is developed to achieve organisational goals.

    D selection, prioritisation and control of an organisation's projects and programmes.

19 Which of the following would best justify the implementation of portfolio management?

    A When more projects that the organisation delivers need to be delivered on time and on budget.

    B When the organisation needs to have a stronger focus on realising the benefits from the projects that it delivers.

    C Where there is a need for the organisation's projects and programmes to be more aligned with its key business objectives.

    D When there is a significant one-off project that needs to be delivered that is critical to the organisation's business continuity.

20 Which is not a key responsibility of a portfolio manager?

    A To ensure that the objective of each project, programme and business-as-usual operation is in line with the organisation's strategic objectives.

    B To prioritise allocation of resources to provide maximum benefit to the portfolio.

    C To define detailed requirements for each project within the portfolio.

    D To coordinate common processes to ensure maximum benefit.

21 Which is a correct statement? A key advantage of portfolio management is that it:

    A allows portfolio managers to focus more on day-to-day routine activities.

    B ensures that any programmes and projects do not impact adversely on business-as-usual.

    C reduces the interference of business-as-usual stakeholders in project work.

    D avoids changes that may impact on business-as-usual activities.

22 What is one of the main goals of portfolio management?

    A To balance the implementation of change initiatives and the maintenance of business-as-usual.

    B To allow portfolio managers to manage more on a day-to-day basis and so improve decision-making.

    C To help each project manager deliver their project into business-as-usual and realise benefits.

    D To reduce the amount of change that is implemented into business-as-usual and so avoid unnecessary impact on operations.

NOW CHECK YOUR ANSWERS AT THE END OF THIS SECTION. YOUR SCORE: /22

2.1.3 Project roles

1 Which of the following statements about the role of project sponsor is false?

   A A project sponsor is an advocate for the project and the change it brings about.
   B A project sponsor writes and owns the project management plan.
   C A project sponsor is able to work across functional boundaries within an organisation.
   D A project sponsor is prepared to commit sufficient time and effort to support the project.

2 Which statement best describes a responsibility of the project sponsor?

   A Monitoring progress and use of the project resources.
   B Analysing the project team's productivity.
   C Ensuring the benefits of the project are realised.
   D Planning project evaluation reviews for lessons learned.

3 What is a key role of the project manager?

   A Coordinating the development of the project management plan.
   B Conducting benefits realisation reviews.
   C Reviewing progress against success criteria and checking that the planned business benefits will be achieved.
   D Authorising any changes to the business case.

4 The group whose remit is to set the strategic direction of a project is commonly known as:

   A the project management team.
   B the primary user group.
   C the steering group.
   D the supplier group.

5 Which stakeholders are likely to form the main part of a project governance board?

   A Project sponsor, project manager and quality manager.
   B Corporate management, project sponsor, quality manager and project office.
   C Sponsor, supplier representative and user representative.
   D Sponsor, project manager and senior project team members.

6 Who in the project is responsible for benefits realisation?

   A The senior management of the organisation.
   B The project manager.
   C The sponsor.
   D The end users.

7 Which of the following roles is primarily responsible for defining goals and creating vision for the operability of the project's outputs?

   A Project sponsor.
   B Product owner.
   C User.
   D Business case owner.

8 What is an example of a project management office activity that would be most likely undertaken to support a project?

   A Developing the project management plan.

   B Developing the business case.

   C Carrying out a health check.

   D Carrying out day-to-day resource management.

9 When effectively implemented, what is one of the key roles of governance?

   A Provide confidence that the business case is the best option for the current circumstances and that there will be no changes as the project is being delivered.

   B Provide confidence that the plans that have been developed will guarantee that the project will be delivered on time and to budget.

   C Provide confidence to all stakeholders that projects are being well managed and the most appropriate financial and technical controls are being exerted.

   D Provide confidence to all project team members that their jobs are secure at least for the period from the project start to the handover.

10 Governance could best be defined as:

   A the framework of authority and accountability that defines and controls the outputs, outcomes and benefits from projects, programmes and portfolios.

   B the framework that structures a review of the project, programme or portfolio and aids in making a decision about whether to continue with the next phase or stage of progress.

   C the framework that is used for selection, prioritisation and control of an organisation's projects and programmes in line with its strategic objectives and capacity to deliver.

   D the framework used by the organisation and approved by the project board at project initiation that allows the definition of the terms of reference for the project.

11 Who is best placed in the project to manage sponsor and user expectations?

   A The senior management team.

   B The project manager.

   C The project management office.

   D The project team.

12 Where in the project life cycle would the project manager typically be appointed?

   A At the start of the concept phase.

   B At the start of the definition phase.

   C At the start of the development phase.

   D At the end of the handover stage.

NOW CHECK YOUR ANSWERS AT THE END OF THIS SECTION. YOUR SCORE: /12

2.1.4 Business case

1 Which of the following best describes a project's business case?

   A The definition of why the project is required and the desired benefits.
   B A statement of what the project will deliver in terms of products/deliverables.
   C The reason why the project sponsor wants the project to proceed.
   D A statement as to how the project fits into the long-term aims of the project sponsor.

2 What information would be expected as content for a business case?

   A A detailed schedule of the project.
   B An outline of the project management team.
   C An outline of the estimated costs of implementing the project.
   D A detailed breakdown of the scope of the project.

3 Which of the following statements about the business case is true?

   A The business case should always be referred to throughout the project.
   B The business case, once written, will never change.
   C The business case becomes the project manager's responsibility, once the project is in the implementation phase.
   D The business case contains key information on how the project will be performed.

4 The responsibility for development and production of the business case is primarily with:

   A the project manager.
   B jointly shared between the project manager and project sponsor.
   C the project sponsor.
   D the project steering group/committee.

5 Which of the following would not be considered to be part of the business case?

   A Safety plan for the project.
   B Implementation options.
   C Stakeholder identification.
   D Business benefits.

6 What is the importance of having a business case?

   A It allows the sponsor to use the document as a baseline to calculate project slippage.
   B It provides an overview of the project team performance at each stage of delivery.
   C It shows how the project manager is performing in delivering the project.
   D It allows the sponsor to decide on project continuity when used at gate reviews.

7 Which one of the following does not describe the prime purpose of the business case?

   A To define the strategic direction for the project.
   B To describe the operational impact of project delivery.
   C To show how the project tasks will be scheduled to achieve the success criteria.
   D To document the benefits of the various options that have been considered.

8 Which of the following is most true of the business case?

  A It provides details of the overarching approach to be taken to move from the current to a future desirable state using a coordinated and structured approach.

  B It evaluates the benefit, cost and risk of alternative project options and provides a rationale for the preferred solution.

  C It demonstrates the relationship between the costs of undertaking a project, initial and recurrent, and the benefits likely to arise from the changed situation, initially and recurrently.

  D It describes each major element in the work breakdown structure (WBS), describing the work content, the resources required, the time frame of the work element and a cost estimate.

9 How does having a business case help an organisation?

  A It provides a documented account of the decisions that have been made, and by whom, in the planning of the project's finances, ensuring the project's compliance with recognised governance standards.

  B It provides an overview of how the project will deliver the scheduled progress over the period agreed between the project manager, sponsor and other key stakeholders associated with the project.

  C It provides a means by which the sponsor can monitor the project manager's performance in relation to the plans documented in the business case and highlight points at which a change of project manager may be necessary.

  D It provides a recognised framework by which project spending proposals can be recorded, reviewed and audited to learn lessons about how efficiently the organisation is deploying funds to achieve its targeted returns.

10 What aspects of benefits realisation would be considered most important to note in the business case?

  A Who is going to be responsible for carrying out each of the project's activities.

  B How the benefits will be realised and measured, and the stakeholders involved.

  C What type of contract is going to be used to procure delivery of the project.

  D Which benefits should be realised first and then the subsequent order.

11 Which statement regarding the purpose of the business case would be most true?

  A Once agreed the business case will become the baseline by which the project will be deployed.

  B It will act as a reference for the project team regarding the specific processes to be used for project delivery.

  C It will determine which stakeholders are most eligible to become members of the steering group.

  D It will be referred to throughout the project in order to make decisions about the continuing viability of the project.

12 What aspect of business case development will assist project management the most?

   A That the sponsor who has developed the business case will also be the sponsor who oversees actual delivery of the project.

   B That the option chosen has taken recognition of how the resultant project is actually going to be managed and delivered.

   C That the project management plan for the project is captured as an appendix of the approved business case.

   D That the business case has sufficient detail to allow the project manager to take over accountability for the financial success of the project.

NOW CHECK YOUR ANSWERS AT THE END OF THIS SECTION. YOUR SCORE: /12

2.1.5 Project life cycles

1 Which of the following is true regarding differences between linear and iterative life cycles?

   A A linear life cycle is best for evolving projects whereas an iterative life cycle is better for more structured projects.

   B A linear life cycle is sequential whereas an iterative life cycle repeats one or more phases.

   C A linear life cycle is always longer in duration whereas an iterative life cycle is always shorter in its duration.

   D A linear life cycle is formally managed by a dedicated project manager whereas management responsibility is shared in an iterative life cycle.

2 A generic linear project life cycle might include the sequence:

   A Definition, concept, design, implementation, transition.

   B Concept, definition, deployment, transition.

   C Planning, deployment, closing, learning, review.

   D Feasibility, planning, deployment, handover, review.

3 One of the main purposes of dividing a project into life cycle phases is to:

   A break the work into controllable blocks in terms of effort and size.

   B ensure the processes are properly maintained.

   C ensure that the workforce is certain of their individual roles.

   D provide a means of producing overall project cost estimates.

4 Implementation of plans and verification of performance is most likely to occur in:

   A the deployment phase.

   B the definition phase.

   C the concept phase.

   D the adoption phase.

5 Which of the following might be a probable cause to consider early project closure?

   A The cost to complete the project is greater than the value to be achieved.

   B The project is on schedule but has spent less than expected.

   C The project is expected to yield greater value than stated in the business case.

   D The project manager has resigned and an immediate replacement is unavailable.

6 Which one of the following statements about the project life cycle is true?

   A The phases in the project life cycle are always the same size.

   B The same processes are used in each of the project life cycle phases.

   C The project life cycle has a number of distinct phases.

   D The project budget is divided equally between each phase of the project life cycle.

7 Where in the project life cycle is benefits realisation most common?

   A The start of deployment.

   B The end of deployment.

   C The end of the concept phase prior to handover.

   D The extended life cycle.

8 What is the main purpose of iterations in an iterative life cycle?

   A To reassure stakeholders that the project will deliver as expected.

   B To progressively elaborate and improve understanding based on client interaction.

   C To allow time for a thorough project management plan to be developed.

   D To ensure that the project manager appointed understands exactly what is required.

9 What is the main benefit of using prototyping, timeboxing or iterative thinking?

   A They offer tested methods for experimentation and risk reduction.

   B They reduce stakeholders' expectations of how they will benefit from the project.

   C They allow the project to develop an extended life cycle.

   D They always deliver the project quicker than planned.

10 What are the likely results of building agile working into a project or programme?

   A Reduced schedule time.

   B Increased cost.

   C Increased efficiency and flexibility.

   D Reduced risk.

11 Which phase of the project life cycle will utilise the new project and enable the acceptance and use of the benefits?

   A adoption.

   B transition.

   C deployment.

   D implementation.

12 What is the main reason for having an extended life cycle?

    A Allow the project to have extra time to ensure that that there is enough capacity to realise benefits.

    B Allow upfront planning for any supplemental activities and incorporate additional considerations for benefits realisation.

    C Allow time for stakeholders to decide how they will use the output to best effect that will realise benefits.

    D Allow extra funding to be applied to the project to ensure that sufficient resources exist to maximise benefits realisation.

NOW CHECK YOUR ANSWERS AT THE END OF THIS SECTION. YOUR SCORE: /12

2.1.6 Project management plan

1 A project management plan could best be described as:

    A an activity on a network diagram.

    B a Gantt chart.

    C a plan for the programme.

    D an overall plan for the project.

2 You have been asked to assist in the development of a project management plan for the project. As a minimum, what should this plan include?

    A A summary of the project acceptance criteria.

    B CVs of all the team members.

    C Details of previous similar projects.

    D Resourcing details for quality reviews.

3 During the consideration of when and how the development of the project management plan should take place, the objectives of carrying out such an exercise can often appear to be uncertain. As a recommendation, the project management plan should be:

    A assembled when all information is available.

    B developed iteratively throughout the early stages of the project.

    C completed in detail before the project is authorised.

    D free from detailed schedule information.

4 To effectively manage the project the range of documentation may appear to be extensive; however, the document that captures the why, what, where, when, how, how much and who for the project is called:

    A the project schedule.

    B the project definition and delivery report.

    C the project feasibility report.

    D the project management plan.

5 Which one of the following statements about the project management plan (PMP) is considered to be the most important condition of compliance to ensure an effective plan is produced?

   A The project team should not contribute to the writing of the PMP.

   B The PMP should be agreed and signed off by both the sponsor and the project manager as a minimum.

   C The sponsor should maintain ownership of the PMP.

   D The PMP is necessary for effective stakeholder management.

6 Which of the following would be considered the main purpose of a project management plan?

   A To provide a documented account of the outcomes of the planning process.

   B To enable agreement between the project sponsor and project manager with regard to project budget, resource requirements and timescale.

   C To provide a record of how the project was planned, for archiving in the organisation's lessons learned.

   D To identify and record the project's intended financial spend over the period of project delivery.

7 What is the agreed reference point that is communicated to stakeholders prior to any work being started?

   A Verified work breakdown structure.

   B Deployment baseline.

   C Configuration record.

   D Business case.

8 Why is it important to produce a project management plan?

   A It shows the benefits expected at the close of the project and the specific stakeholders who are involved.

   B It provides justification for undertaking the project and provides a rationale for the preferred solution.

   C It sets and clarifies the expectations of all stakeholders who are involved in the project delivery.

   D It identifies and establishes the most appropriate means of procuring the component parts or services for the project being delivered.

9 When in the project life cycle should the deployment baseline be formed?

   A Deployment phase.

   B Concept phase.

   C Definition phase.

   D Transition phase.

10 What information would you not expect to see in a project management plan?

   A Quality management plan.

   B Financial feasibility analysis.

   C Risk management plan.

   D Details of scope.

11 How is the deployment baseline used throughout the project?

    A Progress monitoring and implementation of change control.

    B Benefits realisation.

    C Identify options for deployment.

    D Prepare users for delivery of the output into operation.

12 Success criteria can be defined as:

    A measures of success that can be used throughout the project to ensure that it is progressing towards a successful conclusion.

    B management practices that will increase the likelihood of success of a project.

    C the satisfaction of stakeholder needs for the deployment of a project.

    D the value of benefits that are realised when the project delivers its output into business-as-usual.

NOW CHECK YOUR ANSWERS AT THE END OF THIS SECTION. YOUR SCORE: /12

2.2 Planning for success

2.2.1 Stakeholder engagement

1 A project stakeholder could best be described as:

    A a member of the sponsoring organisation's board of directors.

    B a key player who is seeking to maximise control over the project outcome.

    C a person or group who has an interest in or is impacted by the project.

    D a project team member who has the skills necessary to deliver the project.

2 Stakeholder analysis considers three aspects for each stakeholder, which are:

    A their interest in the project, whether or not they can influence the project and whether their attitude to the project is for or against.

    B their level of technical knowledge, whether or not they are able to act as sponsor and whether they are available.

    C their experience, position in the organisational hierarchy and number of resources managed.

    D their interest in the project, whether or not they are a member of the steering group and whether they are likely to resist changes.

3 An example of an external stakeholder group could be:

    A users.

    B a governmental regulatory body.

    C functional managers within the sponsoring organisation.

    D the project team members.

4 One benefit of stakeholder analysis is that:

    A the communication plan becomes unnecessary.

    B the stakeholders who oppose the project the most can be 'cut off' to reduce their negative influence.

    C the communication requirements for each stakeholder can be established.

    D the stakeholders can be removed from any of the decisions that are being planned.

5 Understanding who stakeholders are and their needs is a key duty of:

    A the quality manager.

    B the key users.

    C the project manager.

    D the business sponsor.

6 The main objective of stakeholder management is to establish stakeholder:

    A interests.

    B expectations.

    C influence.

    D engagement.

7 What rule of thumb can be used for ensuring that key stakeholders have been included in the process?

    A Make use of widely available templates and predefined structures to ensure a complete spectrum of stakeholders are identified.

    B Ask the most influential stakeholders to identify who else they think should be involved in the project.

    C Analyse other projects and who their stakeholders are and include them by default.

    D Question whose support or lack of it might significantly influence the success of the project.

8 What is the most likely reason a stakeholder may object to the project?

    A They have a lack of interest in what the project is trying to achieve as they feel it doesn't really affect them.

    B They haven't been involved in choosing what they believe to be a suitable project manager from the candidates available.

    C They have misunderstood what the project is trying to achieve and have had very little communication from the project.

    D They are a stakeholder in another project and currently don't have the time to perform the stakeholder role.

9 What is one of the most important aspects to establish about a stakeholder's interest in the project?

    A Whether it is positive or negative.

    B Whether it is regular or intermittent.

    C Whether it is influenced by the project.

    D Whether it is influenced by other stakeholders.

10 What is essential for ensuring the level of stakeholder engagement is maintained throughout the delivery of the project?

  A Stakeholders communicate with each other.
  B The project management plan is established.
  C An effective communication plan is used.
  D All stakeholders are treated equally.

11 What benefit justifies expending resources to achieve stakeholder engagement?

  A Optimised resource management opportunities.
  B Reduced overall costs of project delivery.
  C Decreased duration of the project schedule.
  D Increased likelihood of the project being accepted.

12 How can the project manager ensure a sound stakeholder environment?

  A Ensure that stakeholders who oppose the project are not involved.
  B Develop an environment where all stakeholders' needs are satisfied.
  C Develop ways of understanding the needs of stakeholders.
  D Ensure that the influence stakeholders have is reduced.

NOW CHECK YOUR ANSWERS AT THE END OF THIS SECTION. YOUR SCORE: /12

2.2.2 Communication

1 Three general categories for interpretation of communication could be described as:

  A email, paper, voice.
  B tactile/visual, auditory, written.
  C telephone, computer, microphone.
  D reception, transmission, interruption.

2 To ensure communication is most likely to be effective in the project, the project manager should:

  A ensure that everyone is copied on all emails.
  B insist on a lower level of paper documents.
  C train project staff in the most up-to-date communication techniques.
  D develop a communication plan.

3 Successful project communications will most likely occur when:

  A the project sponsor takes responsibility for planning all stakeholder communication From the outset.
  B email is the primary method used in order to get information to stakeholders in a speedy and efficient manner.
  C a standard project communication format for reports is used to provide feedback to stakeholders.
  D the different communication needs of each stakeholder group are fully understood.

4 What is likely to be a benefit to a project of having a communication plan?

    A The project is more likely to finish on time.

    B There will be greater adherence to the organisation's governance and standards.

    C The project will be less susceptible to uncontrolled change.

    D There will be more focus on what benefits the project will be delivering.

5 What action can lead to more consistent communication in the project?

    A Only transmitting information that stakeholders have requested, ensuring that any excess information is kept to a minimum.

    B Communication is carried out en masse, ensuring that all stakeholders get all information.

    C Communication is planned in advance and all messages delivered use the approved framework.

    D Communicating information on a one-way basis, reducing the need for stakeholders to waste their time providing feedback.

6 One way that communication could be improved in the project is to:

    A ensure that free-flowing feedback channels are planned into the communication structure.

    B ensure that communication is carried out as much as possible, transmitting as much information as possible.

    C target only those stakeholders who seem to show a valid interest in the project.

    D avoid planning communication too much so that messages are not seen as rigid and overly complex.

7 What is a factor that is important when communicating as part of stakeholder engagement?

    A Planned communication will help to establish the level of interest and power a stakeholder is likely to possess.

    B Planned communication will increase the number of stakeholders who are likely to have an interest in the project.

    C Planned communication will reduce the power of stakeholders who are likely to have an interest in the project.

    D Planned communication is likely to reduce the number of valid stakeholders who have an interest in the project.

8 What could be considered a significant barrier to communication?

    A Use of body language.

    B Having formal meetings.

    C Attitudes, emotions and prejudices.

    D Use of informal communication channels.

9 If planning a meeting where there were likely to be stakeholders with widely different levels of knowledge and experience attending, what practical proactive measure could the project manager take to reduce the impact of communication barriers?

A Ensure that the meeting room was reserved for a longer period than normal.

B Have a number of meetings where some are technical and some non-technical.

C Aim for a common level of discussion, avoiding too technical discussions.

D Ensure that a glossary of technical terms was made available in advance.

10 What might be considered a disadvantage of virtual communication?

A Digital communication links never seem to work as required.

B Communication being misunderstood.

C There is no method for providing feedback.

D This method of communication tends to be time-consuming.

11 Which factor is likely to have the biggest influence over the success of communication?

A The size of the communication plan.

B The method of communication chosen.

C The age range of those communicating.

D The type of project being delivered.

12 What is the main aim of the communication plan?

A To increase the chances of achieving effective engagement.

B To comply with the structure of the project management plan.

C To identify the skills necessary to deliver a project.

D To increase the likelihood of benefits realisation.

NOW CHECK YOUR ANSWERS AT THE END OF THIS SECTION. YOUR SCORE: /12

2.2.3 Risk and issue management

1 While providing support to the project and attending a risk management workshop, the following statements were noted. Which one of these could be considered a risk to a project?

   A We have never done a project of this kind before.
   B We might not have sufficient people with the right experience to undertake the project.
   C We always find that design verification takes longer than planned.
   D We have never worked in that country before.

2 On examining a particular risk in the project there is some uncertainty among the project team about how important this risk is to the project. How would you advise the team on how the significance of the risk is to be determined?

   A By assessing its probability of occurrence.
   B By assessing its impact on project objectives.
   C By assessing both its probability of occurrence and its impact on project objectives.
   D By assessing its effect on the business case.

3 What is the main benefit of using a risk register in the project?

   A It records risks, their impact and the responses being adopted.
   B It records risk ownership and how issues are being managed.
   C It assesses the impact and probability of risks taking place.
   D It directs the team in how the management of risk in the project should be conducted.

4 A member of your team has described being involved in a risk event. Which one of the following would best describe such an event?

   A An action or set of actions to reduce the probability or impact of a threat, or to increase the probability or impact of an opportunity.
   B The plan for the response to risks.
   C An uncertain event or set of circumstances that if realised would have an effect on project objectives.
   D A risk identification workshop.

5 Which one of the following statements about project risk is true?

   A Risk is always beneficial to the project.
   B Risk is neither beneficial nor detrimental to the project.
   C Risk can be beneficial or detrimental to the project.
   D Risk is always detrimental to the project.

6 A typical risk management process would follow the steps:

   A identification, analysis, response, closure.
   B assessment, analysis, closure, response.
   C assessment, planning, managing, response.
   D identification, planning, response, closure.

7   Who would be typically described as the person or organisation best placed to deal with a risk?

   A Risk manager.

   B Sponsor.

   C Project sponsor.

   D Risk owner.

8   As part of the risk management process, the capture of threats and opportunities to the project objectives are referred to as:

   A risk assessment.

   B risk avoidance.

   C risk exposure.

   D risk identification.

9   Which one of the following would be expected to form the main part of a risk analysis?

   A Deciding on the approach to project risk management.

   B Evaluating the risk in terms of severity and relative importance.

   C Deciding on how to respond to the risk and who should implement the response.

   D Deciding whether the risk is a threat or opportunity.

10 The implementation of risk management on a project requires a cost allocation from the project budget. Which statement describes the most representative return from such an investment?

   A There will be a benefit to the project if potential opportunities are realised.

   B The cost of dealing with a risk should it occur is usually greater than the cost of managing that risk.

   C Risk management in the project facilitates team-building.

   D It allows the organisation to assure stakeholders of project compliance with regard to risk management.

11 Which of the following descriptions particularly identifies a risk?

   A An unplanned delay to the project.

   B A current problem that will result in the project going over budget.

   C An uncertain event that, if it occurs, will have an effect on one or more of the project objectives.

   D A current problem that will result in the project being delayed.

12 Which one of these categories would best represent project issues?

   A Uncertain events that may or may not occur.

   B Opportunities that occur through change control.

   C Problems that the project manager has to deal with on a day-to-day basis.

   D Threats to the project which cannot be resolved by the project manager.

13 What is the likely decision to arise from the response stage of the risk management process?

    A Whether to proceed with the project or recommend termination.

    B Whether the process being used is robust enough for the project being undertaken.

    C Whether to proactively invest to bring the exposure to risk within tolerable levels.

    D Whether to use brainstorming or a workshop to decide on the best response.

14 For successful risk identification to take place what must the project team know as a minimum?

    A Skills of the team delivering the project.

    B Project objectives.

    C Amount of time allowed for risk identification to take place.

    D Location of the venue where risk identification will take place.

15 What defining characteristic from those listed below particularly typifies an issue?

    A A major problem that was unexpected and now requires the attention of the whole project team.

    B A major problem that can only be addressed by the project sponsor.

    C A major problem that may happen in the future.

    D A major problem that requires a formal process of escalation.

16 Which one of the following is not an example of a project issue?

    A There are no suppliers that can meet our specification.

    B We may not be able to finish on time.

    C The project is going to be late.

    D A key phase of the project is taking longer than expected.

17 Throughout the life of the project, issues that are raised are best recorded in the:

    A quality register.

    B issue register.

    C change register.

    D risk register.

18 What must happen when an issue is likely to result in a change of scope?

    A The issue owner is consulted.

    B A decision regarding the issue is deferred.

    C The issue is rejected and the owner is informed.

    D The issue is progressed through change control.

19 How should issues be prioritised?

    A The time order in which the issues occurred.

    B The impact on success criteria and benefits.

    C The relative seniority of the issue owner.

    D The relationship with a relevant risk.

20 A typical issue management process could follow the steps:

    A identification, escalation, action, resolution.

    B assessment, escalation, closure, resolution.

    C assessment, planning, action, response.

    D identification, planning, response, resolution.

NOW CHECK YOUR ANSWERS AT THE END OF THIS SECTION. YOUR SCORE: /20

2.2.4 Quality management

1 How is 'quality' best defined?

    A The process of evaluating overall project performance on a regular basis to provide confidence that the project will satisfy the relevant quality standards.

    B The fitness for purpose or the degree of conformance of the outputs of a process, or the process itself, to requirements.

    C A discipline for ensuring the outputs, the benefits and the processes by which they are delivered meet stakeholder requirements and are fit for purpose.

    D The satisfaction of stakeholder needs measured by the success criteria as identified and agreed at the start of the project.

2 While carrying out quality management for the project, you have been assigned the task of determining the quality standards that are applicable and how they should apply. Which part of quality management would best describe this activity?

    A Quality planning.

    B Quality assurance.

    C Total quality.

    D Quality control.

3 To be considered effective, how should quality management be used in the project?

    A To ensure compliance.

    B To ensure quality standards are met.

    C To ensure the required process needs of stakeholders are met.

    D To ensure both the project outputs and the processes meet the required needs of stakeholders.

4 During project deployment, which process will provide confidence that the project will satisfy the relevant quality standards?

    A Quality assurance for the project.

    B Strategic business planning for quality (SBPQ).

    C Total quality planning.

    D Total quality management (TQM).

5 What is the most likely result of providing effective quality management in the project?

   A The project outputs will have been delivered.

   B Conformance of the outputs and processes to requirements will have resulted in a product that is fit for purpose.

   C The project management plan will have been followed.

   D Customer expectations will have been exceeded with both outputs and processes.

6 You have been asked to review the project's quality management plan and in particular the elements of the plan most relevant to quality control. Which one of the following will be your primary focus for consideration?

   A The development of a strategy for the management of quality in the project.

   B Supplying the client with evidence of control to ISO 9000:2000.

   C A review of whether underlying processes and ways of working are leading towards product deliverables of the right quality.

   D The agreed methods of inspection, measurement and testing to verify that the project outputs meet acceptance criteria defined during quality planning.

7 What would be the most direct symptom of poor quality in the project?

   A The project not using compliant management processes.

   B The customer refusing to take delivery of the finished product.

   C The failure of a quality assurance audit.

   D The project finishing over budget.

8 The characteristics of a product that determine whether it meets certain requirements are known as the:

   A product criteria.

   B acceptance criteria.

   C quality criteria.

   D success criteria.

9 The question 'Is the project actually following the processes and procedures as set out in the quality plan?' would be answered by:

   A quality alignment

   B quality control

   C quality assurance

   D quality improvement

10 Which of the following provide(s) the project manager with a formal overview of project quality?

   A Design reviews.

   B Project definition reports.

   C Quality audits.

   D Historical experience.

11 When should test plans for quality control be agreed?

   A During quality planning.

   B When the live product is available for test.

   C At the end of the project.

   D Prior to handover of the output.

12 Inspection, measurement and testing to verify that the project outputs meet acceptance criteria is an example of quality:

   A reporting.

   B control.

   C assurance.

   D planning.

13 A review most closely linked to the phases of the project life cycle could be described as a:

   A gate review.

   B learning review.

   C handover review.

   D audit review.

14 One benefit of a gate review process is:

   A it allows learning from one phase of the project to be passed on to the next phase.

   B it stops projects that no longer meet the organisation's needs.

   C it allows procurement to be planned into the project life cycle.

   D it allows the project team to plan delivery of the next phase.

15 Which one of the following would best describe a post-project review?

   A It is a personal appraisal for each team member on completion of the project.

   B It appraises the products of the project.

   C It considers all aspects of the management of the project.

   D It involves only the project implementation team.

16 The post-project review report should be:

   A included in the project plan for the next similar project.

   B restricted in circulation in case it contains critical information.

   C archived for use in a future audit of project management processes.

   D available to all project managers within the organisation.

17 Which of the following would be considered a valid objective for the post-project review?

   A Plan the next project for the project team.

   B Make proposals for the operation of the project deliverables.

   C Improve future estimating accuracy.

   D Plan how to complete the objectives of the project.

18 Which of the following would not be considered part of the post-project review?

    A Evaluation of the benefits of the project.

    B Identification of the problems that arose and their likely causes.

    C Review of the project's performance against the success criteria.

    D Review of how the team worked together to solve problems and issues.

19 What is the main objective of an audit?

    A Provide assurance to the project sponsor that the project is going to finish on time and within budget.

    B Provide feedback to the project manager with regard to their performance in managing the project.

    C Provide assurance to the sponsor that the project is being managed using the agreed governance and process.

    D Provide a report of the current status of the project regarding cost and schedule performance.

20 When is it best to carry out a benefit review?

    A At 6–12 months after handover.

    B At various stages prior to handover.

    C At the concept phase when developing the business case.

    D At various stages through deployment.

NOW CHECK YOUR ANSWERS AT THE END OF THIS SECTION. YOUR SCORE: /20

2.2.5 Scope management

1 What aspect is important to clarify when conducting scope definition?

    A The number of products contained in the PBS.

    B The boundaries and interfaces with adjacent projects.

    C Who is going to perform the work.

    D When the work is going to be performed.

2 How are outputs best described?

    A The changed circumstances or behaviour that results from their use.

    B The work packages developed in the WBS for the project.

    C The realisation of benefits at the end of the project.

    D The tangible or intangible products typically delivered by a project.

3 The combination of which two structures creates the responsibility assignment matrix (RAM)?

    A OBS and CBS.

    B OBS and WBS.

    C PBS and CBS.

    D WBS and CBS.

4 Scope management in an iterative life cycle would ensure that:

    A the 'must-have' requirements are given the top priority for delivery.

    B the scope is identified at a deeper level in the project.

    C all stakeholders get what they want from the project.

    D areas of the project that will be delivered are fully agreed.

5 If using an iterative life cycle what actions might be necessary for scope items that are not considered as 'must-have'?

    A They need to be given a special priority to ensure that they are definitely delivered.

    B They should have the best resources allocated to ensure they are most efficiently delivered.

    C The project could be extended if the delivery of these requirements were proving more difficult than expected.

    D They would be sacrificed if at any time the project was predicted to go over budget or be late.

6 In a RACI coding format, what does 'A' stand for?

    A Available.

    B Authorised.

    C Accountable.

    D Acceptable.

7 What is the main objective of a RAM?

    A To provide a clear and concise summary of tasks or deliverables and the specific responsibilities defined.

    B To provide an outline of the reporting structure to assist in day-to-day management of the project.

    C To provide an outline of the scope of the project and the specific deliverables that have been agreed for the project.

    D To provide an outline of the specific costs of the project and which key deliverables they are allocated to.

8 How is it determined whether a deliverable conforms to its requirements and configuration information?

    A A configuration management plan is produced.

    B A configuration identification reference is allocated to the deliverable.

    C A configuration verification audit is performed.

    D A status accounting report is produced.

9 A key output of a well-controlled configuration management process is:

    A documented traceability between versions of each configuration item.

    B that the project is most likely to meet its success criteria.

    C documented evidence of all project changes: proposed, authorised, rejected or deferred.

    D an agreed point after which no further changes to scope will be considered.

10 Configuration management could best be described as:

A the process through which all requests to change the approved baseline of a project are captured, evaluated and then approved, rejected or deferred.

B the system that ensures that all changes to configuration items are controlled and the interrelationships between items are identified.

C the technical and administrative activities concerned with the creation, maintenance, controlled change and quality control of the scope of work.

D a report of the current status and history of all changes to the configuration, together with a complete record of what has happened to the configuration to date.

11 Which of the following would be considered part of a configuration management process?

A Initiating, identifying, assessing, planning, responding.

B Planning, identifying, controlling, status accounting, auditing.

C Scheduling, baselining, controlling, responding, closing.

D Planning, auditing, monitoring, controlling, closing.

12 Configuration management would be used to:

A ensure the required materials are in stock when needed.

B help the impact of a change request to be fully assessed.

C help configuration within IT projects.

D ensure that a work breakdown structure can be completed.

13 Who is primarily responsible for configuration management in the project?

A Project manager.

B Risk manager.

C Quality manager.

D Project team.

14 The prime purpose of configuration management is to:

A ensure the traceability and integrity of the delivered product or products.

B minimise the impact of changes on the scope of the project.

C ensure that the final product meets the needs of the business as defined by key stakeholders.

D maximise the impact of agreed enhancements to the project deliverables.

15 What is the key benefit of having configuration management in the project?

A It allows a thorough assessment of the factors that are most likely to affect the change.

B It is a means to justify to the customer variances from the original objectives.

C It ensures that the delivered product most closely meets the needs of the customer.

D It manages the impact of change to the project scope.

16 What is the main reason for an initial high-level review of a change request?

   A To consider whether the change is feasible to evaluate at this stage.

   B To establish who might be the best stakeholders to be involved in the change.

   C To ensure that the change request is considered as soon as possible.

   D To implement the necessary actions to ensure the change has a smooth implementation.

17 What action is essential after a change has been approved?

   A The highlights of the change are communicated directly to the sponsor.

   B The actual impact of the change is assessed.

   C The next change requested is reviewed as quickly as possible.

   D The related plans must be updated to reflect the change.

18 A formally constituted group of stakeholders responsible for approving or rejecting changes to the project baselines is referred to as the:

   A change management committee.

   B change authority.

   C change control board.

   D change implementation group.

19 Which of the following would be considered most important when carrying out a detailed evaluation of a change?

   A Impact of change on baseline, risks and business case.

   B The number of extra people required to deliver the change.

   C How the change will be reported when it is implemented into the project.

   D The configuration requirements of the change when implemented into the project.

20 When no other changes are being considered to the project, this is usually termed as a:

   A scope verification.

   B change freeze.

   C consolidated baseline.

   D configuration control.

NOW CHECK YOUR ANSWERS AT THE END OF THIS SECTION. YOUR SCORE: /20

2.3 Achieving results

2.3.1 Estimating

1 What aspect of the project will have greatest influence on the estimating method being used?

 A The point in the life cycle where the estimate is being carried out.

 B The overall budgeted value of the project being estimated.

 C Whether the project is likely to proceed or not.

 D The amount of acceptable estimating tolerance that exists.

2 What is the prime advantage of using a parametric estimating method?

 A Accuracy.

 B Ability to deal with detailed information.

 C Independence from historical data.

 D Speed.

3 Which of the following statements about estimating is true?

 A Post-project reviews are a prime source of estimating data.

 B An estimated cost for a project must be within 10% to be of any use.

 C If you cannot estimate task durations to within 20% there is no point in developing a schedule.

 D The project manager should always add 10% to other people's duration estimates to allow for natural optimism.

4 The project you are working on has chosen to produce an estimate using a detailed work breakdown structure (WBS). What estimating method is this approach commonly known as?

 A Comparative estimating.

 B Bottom-up/analytical estimating.

 C Strategic estimating.

 D Parametric estimating.

5 The concept that describes how estimating accuracy changes through the project life cycle is termed:

 A estimating risk.

 B estimating funnel.

 C normal values.

 D parametric estimating.

6 What is the estimating method that uses data from a similar project as the basis for the estimate?

 A Evaluative estimating.

 B Risk-based estimating.

 C Analogous estimating.

 D Analytical estimating.

7   When the project progresses through the life cycle, which one of the following aspects would be expected to occur?

   A   The accuracy of the estimate reduces and the level of contingency requirement increases.

   B   The accuracy of the estimate increases and the level of contingency requirement reduces.

   C   The accuracy and level of contingency requirement both increase.

   D   The accuracy and level of contingency requirement both reduce.

8   What is one of the main features of using the analogous method of estimating?

   A   The individual group members use a statistical relationship between historic data and other variables to calculate an estimate.

   B   The task of producing the estimates will be delegated to those who are actually going to deliver the individual pieces of work or work packages.

   C   The individual group members who are tasked with providing the estimates do this in isolation from each other.

   D   The individual group members identify a previously delivered project of the same size, complexity and delivery method.

9   What is a likely benefit of re-estimating throughout the project life cycle?

   A   The project will be much more economically viable.

   B   The business case is justified to a greater degree.

   C   Overall project duration is reduced.

   D   Reduction in contingency reserves is achieved.

10   What estimating method is most commonly used in the definition phase of the project life cycle?

   A   Analogous.

   B   Analytical.

   C   Parametric.

   D   Statistical.

11   When in the project life cycle might analogous estimating be most commonly used?

   A   Transition.

   B   Concept.

   C   Deployment.

   D   Definition.

12   What factor creates the effect of the estimating funnel?

   A   Project team getting to know each other better.

   B   Utilisation of learning and experience.

   C   Project scope increasing in cost.

   D   Use of a linear life cycle.

NOW CHECK YOUR ANSWERS AT THE END OF THIS SECTION. YOUR SCORE: /12

2.3.2 Resource scheduling and optimisation

1 The critical path on a project network is:

A the shortest path in duration through the network.

B the path with the most float.

C the path with the most activities on it.

D the longest path in duration through the network.

2 In the network diagram below, which is the critical path?

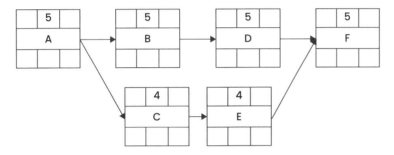

A A, C, E, F.

B A, B, D, F.

C A, C, D, F.

D A, B, E, F.

3 In the above network diagram, which of the activities have total float?

A C and E.

B B and D.

C A only.

D E only.

4 The diagram below shows the relationship between task A and task B.

According to this diagram the dependency shown is an example of:

A Finish to start.

B Finish to finish.

C Start to finish.

D Start to start.

5 Which of the following best describes the concept of total float?

    A The value of the earliest finish of an activity subtracted from the latest finish of the previous activity.

    B The value of the latest finish of an activity subtracted from the earliest start of the same activity.

    C The amount an activity can slip without affecting the overall duration of the project.

    D The amount an activity can slip without affecting the start of the next activity.

6 In a situation where time becomes more important than cost, the project manager should first attempt to:

    A remove resources from critical tasks.

    B perform time-limited scheduling (smoothing).

    C redefine the critical path.

    D perform resource-limited smoothing (levelling).

7 To maintain the scheduled duration when resources are limited, resource levelling should first attempt to:

    A not exceed the predetermined end date.

    B schedule activities within the limits of their float.

    C extend the activity duration.

    D minimise the use of overtime.

The Gantt chart below should be used for answers to questions 8, 9 and 10. It shows the scheduling of seven tasks (A–G) and their daily allocation of resources over a nine-day period. Activities B and F have total float to the extent indicated by the dotted lines.

8 Which of the possible actions would be considered the best application of resource smoothing?

    A Double the amount of resources applied to activity B, reducing its duration to 1 day.

    B Delay activity F to start on day 5 and finish on day 7, reducing to 1 resource per day.

    C Extend the overall schedule duration by 3 days and start the project on day 3.

    D Double the amount of resources applied to activity E, reducing its duration to 1 day.

9 If the total number of resources available is limited to 6 per day, what would be the most efficient way to deal with this constraint?

   A Increase the project budget to acquire additional resources.
   B Extend the overall project duration by 3 days.
   C Move activities B and F to the extent of their float.
   D Move activity F only to start on day 5.

10 If resource levelling was being considered to be applied to the schedule, which activities should be initially considered for this technique?

   A All activities would be considered.
   B Activities B and F would be initially considered.
   C Activities A, C, D, E and G would be initially considered.
   D There is not enough information provided to make such a decision.

11 Procurement could be described as:

   A an outline of the deliverables required by the project.
   B a process by which the resources required by the project are acquired.
   C an outline of the resources required for the project.
   D a definition of who should be the best supplier of goods to the project.

12 Preparation of contracts, selection and acquisition of suppliers, and management of the contracts would be items recorded in the:

   A responsibility matrix
   B work breakdown structure
   C business case
   D procurement strategy

13 One key principle a project manager should follow when carrying out procurement is to:

   A ensure the same suppliers are used in each project to maintain consistency.
   B always use the supplier who will offer the lowest price.
   C always bring in specialist help for support.
   D always use an objective process when selecting suppliers.

14 Which of the following would best describe a contract?

   A An agreement made between two or more parties that creates legally binding obligations between them.
   B An invitation for a supplier to tender at the lowest price.
   C A stage or work package carried out by a chosen supplier.
   D An accepted completed work package.

15 When acquiring goods or services for the project, what might be the most important question for the project manager to raise with the sponsor with regard to the contract?

   A How many suppliers from the market might be willing to submit a tender response.

   B Whether the previous supplier to the project can also be used for the project currently being planned.

   C How much risk to retain in the project and how much to share with suppliers in the supply chain.

   D How much previous experience the organisation has with the suppliers that are currently being considered.

NOW CHECK YOUR ANSWERS AT THE END OF THIS SECTION. YOUR SCORE: /15

2.3.3 Information management and reporting

1 The prime role of a project information management system when reporting information is to:

   A Provide information to the sponsor as and when required.

   B Make decisions about control and coordination of the project.

   C Report on all detailed aspects of the project.

   D Support the decision-making process.

2 Project progress reporting is for the benefit of:

   A the project manager.

   B the project sponsor.

   C the project management team.

   D the project support office.

3 The project manager will be expected to produce reports containing which of the following information?

   A Progress against schedule, expenditure against budget and performance against quality plan.

   B Feasibility of the project options currently being delivered.

   C Business case progress and the risks that will have an impact on its achievement.

   D How benefits are going to be realised once the project has been delivered.

4 The main purpose of project progress reporting is to ensure that:

   A the same information is sent to all stakeholders.

   B the project uses the methods of communication required by the sponsor.

   C the project communicates to stakeholders in the most effective way possible.

   D the project complies with the organisation's information management policies.

5 Reports that are produced only when things are not going to plan are termed:

   A Risk reports.

   B Progress reports.

   C Exception reports.

   D Issue reports.

6 When in the project would it be most likely for archiving of project documentation to take place?

    A After a baseline plan has been created.

    B During project closure.

    C When the scope has been verified by the users.

    D After completion of each phase of the project.

7 Which of the following could be considered the main purpose of project progress reporting?

    A To allow teams and stakeholders to determine whether the project is likely to deliver what is required.

    B To allow stakeholders to judge the degree of project management performance being applied.

    C To ensure the provision of accurate and timely information for teams and stakeholders to keep track of deliverables.

    D To assure stakeholders that the degree of compliance of the project to standard operating practice is acceptable.

8 How might day-to-day information received from teams be used in the project?

    A To provide evidence to the sponsor that the project should not be terminated.

    B Sent to all stakeholders in the project.

    C To support valuations of work performed and related payments.

    D To build a robust project archive.

9 How should the project manager avoid the 'send to all' syndrome?

    A Only send information to those stakeholders who have specifically asked for it.

    B Avoid sending information to most stakeholders.

    C Reduce the amount of information to a bare minimum.

    D Ensure that there is sufficient interaction between information management and communication planning.

10 What must the project manager consider most when planning the destruction of information?

    A That information should be destroyed but a master copy must always be kept on file.

    B That destruction occurs in line with legislative compliance.

    C That there is no need to destroy information after a five-year period.

    D That information stored on digital media doesn't need to be destroyed.

NOW CHECK YOUR ANSWERS AT THE END OF THIS SECTION. YOUR SCORE: /10

2.3.4 Leadership and teamwork

1 Which one of the following statements is true about work that is delegated by the project manager to key team members?

   A The project manager would no longer control the work.

   B The work must be approved by senior line management.

   C It does not reduce the project manager's accountability for that work.

   D It can be carried out without recourse to other ongoing project work.

2 In order to build an effective team, the project manager should:

   A organise 'off-site' team-building events.

   B focus on team selection techniques.

   C ensure that the team members are situated at the same site.

   D clearly define roles and responsibilities.

3 Which one of the following characteristics would best describe an effective team?

   A A group of specialist individuals working on key tasks within the project.

   B A number of people working on both business-as-usual activities and project work.

   C A number of people working collaboratively towards the same goal.

   D A group of people working on a number of different projects within the organisation.

4 Which one of the following aspects would be most important for the project manager to consider in their approach to building and maintaining a team?

   A Let new team members find their own level within the team.

   B Provide focus by cutting links with departments during the project.

   C Ensure the effective induction of new members to the team.

   D Try to ensure that all team members have a similar personality.

5 A leader who ensures that requirements are agreed and that the rewards and penalties for achievement, or lack of it, are understood, could be described as a:

   A transformational leader.

   B hierarchical leader.

   C situational leader.

   D transactional leader.

6 Which one of the following would best describe the most effective leadership ability?

   A The ability to provide inspiration and empowerment to team members.

   B The ability to have a thorough technical expertise in aspects of the project.

   C The ability to communicate clear objectives to team members.

   D The ability to be flexible and sensitive to each individual team member's needs.

7 What is the key purpose of leadership?

   A Provide ongoing support and personal development to individual team members.

   B Develop the technical strategy to achieve business objectives.

   C Establish vision and direction, to influence and align others towards a common purpose.

   D Establish and maintain control over how the project team performs tasks.

8 What aspect can cause a team to move from performing to forming (i.e. backwards)?

   A Change.
   B Risk.
   C Delegation.
   D Monitoring and control.

9 According to Belbin, there are three aspects of personality orientation to consider when developing a team, which are:

   A theory X, theory Y and theory Z.
   B motivated, experienced and skilful.
   C action, social and thinking.
   D project, task and team.

10 How can a project manager best use models to assist team development?

   A To help them evaluate who should be rewarded most in the next team review.
   B To help them define the key technical skills that team members need to perform.
   C To help them decide who they don't want in their team.
   D To help them understand the social dynamics between team members.

11 What single aspect can increase the effectiveness of a leader?

   A Knowing who to recruit into the team.
   B Knowing when to alter their leadership style.
   C Knowing when to stop trying to achieve objectives.
   D Knowing how high to set the monthly team targets.

12 What might be the most appropriate leadership style in a highly critical situation?

   A Coaching.
   B Directing.
   C Delegating.
   D Engaging.

NOW CHECK YOUR ANSWERS AT THE END OF THIS SECTION. YOUR SCORE: /12

3.1.1 Short quizzes answers

Check your answers in each section. For any that are not correct, read over that section again and ensure that you more fully understand the subject area.

Section 2 – Short quizzes answers

2.1 Introducing projects

2.1.1 Project environment

1 A	**2** C	**3** A	**4** A	**5** D	**6** B
7 A	**8** C	**9** B	**10** A	**11** C	**12** B

2.1.2 Project, programme and portfolio management

1 D	**2** B	**3** D	**4** D	**5** B	**6** A
7 C	**8** D	**9** C	**10** A	**11** A	**12** D
13 C	**14** A	**15** B	**16** A	**17** B	**18** D
19 C	**20** C	**21** B	**22** A		

2.1.3 Project roles

1 B	**2** C	**3** A	**4** C	**5** C	**6** C
7 B	**8** C	**9** C	**10** A	**11** B	**12** B

2.1.4 Business case

1 A	**2** C	**3** A	**4** C	**5** A	**6** D
7 C	**8** B	**9** S	**10** B	**11** D	**12** B

2.1.5 Project life cycles

1 B	**2** B	**3** A	**4** A	**5** A	**6** C
7 D	**8** B	**9** A	**10** C	**11** A	**12** B

2.1.6 Project management plan

1 D	**2** A	**3** B	**4** D	**5** B	**6** B
7 B	**8** C	**9** C	**10** B	**11** A	**12** C

2.2 Planning for success

2.2.1 Stakeholder engagement

1 C	**2** A	**3** B	**4** C	**5** C	**6** D
7 D	**8** C	**9** A	**10** C	**11** D	**12** C

2.2.2 Communication

1 B	**2** D	**3** D	**4** B	**5** C	**6** A
7 A	**8** C	**9** D	**10** B	**11** B	**12** A

2.2.3 Risk and issue management

1 B	**2** C	**3** A	**4** C	**5** C	**6** A
7 D	**8** D	**9** B	**10** B	**11** C	**12** D
13 C	**14** B	**15** D	**16** B	**17** B	**18** D
19 B	**20** A				

2.2.4 Quality management

1 B	**2** A	**3** D	**4** A	**5** B	**6** D
7 B	**8** B	**9** C	**10** C	**11** A	**12** B
13 A	**14** B	**15** C	**16** D	**17** C	**18** A
19 C	**20** A				

2.2.5 Scope management

1 B	**2** D	**3** B	**4** A	**5** D	**6** C
7 A	**8** C	**9** A	**10** C	**11** B	**12** B
13 A	**14** A	**15** D	**16** A	**17** D	**18** C
19 A	**20** B				

2.3 Achieving results

2.3.1 Estimating

1 A	2 A	3 A	4 B	5 B	6 C
7 B	8 D	9 D	10 B	11 B	12 B

2.3.2 Resource scheduling and optimisation

1 D	2 B	3 A	4 B	5 C	6 B
7 B	8 B	9 D	10 B	11 B	12 D
13 D	14 A	15 C			

2.3.3 Information management and reporting

1 D	2 C	3 A	4 C	5 C	6 B
7 C	8 C	9 D	10 B		

2.3.4 Leadership and teamwork

1 C	2 D	3 C	4 C	5 D	6 A
7 C	8 A	9 C	10 D	11 B	12 B

Your results

There are 215 questions in total. Add up your marks for each section. To pass the PFQ examination you will need to get 60% correct. For these example questions, that would be 129 out of 215. If you have achieved a greater score than 129, congratulations, you should consider yourself to be exam ready.

Next, have a go at the exam practice paper in the following section.

If you have gained less than 129, review each subject area. It is likely that there are only one or two areas where you need to do a little more work to get you ready for the exam.

Refer to the candidate guidance provided by APM.

3.2 Exam practice questions

The questions outlined in this section will give you some insight into the types and structure of questions that could be seen in the PFQ exam. Your paper will have 60 questions, which will be drawn from any of the 10 learning outcomes and related subject areas contained within this guide. Answer each of the questions and then check the answers at the end of the section.

Use this exercise to practise prior to actually sitting the exam.

Specification for the APM Project Fundamentals Qualification exam

1 Context

The APM Project Fundamentals Qualification will give candidates the ideal start in the profession, providing them with a fundamental awareness of project management principles and terminology.

2 Exam overview

The exam is based upon the learning outcomes and assessment criteria specified in the APM Project Fundamentals Qualification syllabus.

The APM Project Fundamentals Qualification exam:

- is of one hour' duration, which provides sufficient time to read all questions
- contains 60 compulsory multiple-choice questions, each of an equal level of demand

3 Exam instructions to candidates

Instructions given to the candidates are included in the Guide for Candidates which is available on the APM website: www.apm.org.uk.

4 Specification for an APM Project Fundamentals Qualification exam (online/paper)

Compilation of an APM Project Fundamentals Qualification question paper is validated to ensure that:

- each question paper contains questions across the entire syllabus
- the questions forming each paper are drawn from the full range of learning outcomes to reduce the chance of overlap between individual questions
- the order of questions is randomised rather than following the order within the syllabus
- all assessment criteria examined have equal priority
- no single assessment criterion is examined significantly more than any other
- the frequency of the correct answer being A, B, C or D is **not** equal in any one paper
- the order of A, B, C and D as correct answers does *not* follow a pattern

5 Allocation of marks

Within this paper:

- each question is worth 1 mark
- the absence of an answer will score 0
- multiple answers to one question will score 0

6 Pass mark

The pass mark is 60%* of the available marks, i.e. 36 correct questions out of 60.

*This may be changed on the recommendation of the Senior Examiner Team during the lifetime of the qualification.

7 Each question that appears on the question paper:

- will take the average candidate no more than one minute to read and answer
- is appropriate for the target audience for the APM Project Fundamentals Qualification
- is unambiguous
- stands alone and does not rely on an answer from another question that appears in the exam paper

8 Question and answer formats and wording

- All possible answers within a single question will be about the same length.
- Similar grammar will be used for all possible answers within a question.
- Questions and answers will be written in the third person and will be clear and concise.
- Questions may include a diagram, on which the question is based, e.g. an extract from a network diagram.
- Questions will avoid repeated use of terms and phrases.

Section 3 – Sample paper

APM Project Fundamentals Qualification – examination paper

Time allowed: 1 hour.

Answer all 60 multiple-choice questions

Provide only one answer per question.

Question 1

Which of the following is **not** a stage in an issue resolution process?

a   Share the issue with stakeholders.

b   Track the issue to closure.

c   Escalate to the sponsor.

d   Apply change control.

Question 2

Which of the following are challenges for a project manager developing and leading a project team?

1   Issues and incompatibility among team members.

2   Getting the right skills and attributes among team members.

3   Co-location of team members in the same geographic area.

4   Lack of accountability of team members.

a   1, 2 and 3.

b   1, 2 and 4.

c   1, 3 and 4.

d   2, 3 and 4.

Question 3

Which of the following is an activity in a typical change control process?

a   Recommendation.

b   Justification.

c   Planning.

d   Continuous improvement.

Question 4

The purpose of quality assurance is to:

a   provide confidence the project will satisfy the relevant quality standards.

b   determine a set of procedures and standards for project management.

c   inspect, measure and test deliverables and processes.

d   define the scope and specifics of a project's deliverables.

Question 5

A project manager might use a PESTLE analysis in order to:

a mitigate all possible risks to the project.
b identify and mitigate factors that may affect the project.
c control technological change during the project.
d consider team social roles in early stages of the project.

Question 6

Which of the following are phases in an iterative project life cycle?

1 Concept.
2 Feasibility.
3 Deployment.
4 Development.

a 3 and 4 only.
b 1, 2 and 3.
c 1 and 2 only.
d 2, 3 and 4.

Question 7

Which of the following is the responsibility of a project manager?

a Ensuring a project is aligned to the organisation's strategy.
b Focusing on project benefits and aligning priorities.
c Achieving the project's success criteria.
d Improving process, tools and techniques used in a project.

Question 8

To develop and establish a proper communication plan within a project, the project manager needs to consider which type of analysis?

a Budget.
b Stakeholder.
c Resource.
d Schedule.

Question 9

Which of the following is a responsibility of the project sponsor?

a Creating a project cost breakdown structure.
b Authoring the project management plan.
c Creating a project work breakdown structure.
d Owning the project business case.

Question 10

Portfolio management includes prioritising:

a   projects and/or programmes that contribute directly to the organisation's strategic objectives.

b   projects with exceptionally high returns on investment.

c   projects and programmes over business-as-usual.

d   projects which maximise change over those which maximise investment.

Question 11

Which of the following actions would **not** help a team leader influence the performance of their team?

a   Creating an exclusive environment.

b   Providing clear roles and responsibilities.

c   Promoting openness and honesty.

d   Developing a trusting relationship.

Question 12

One difference between a project and business-as-usual is:

a   projects achieve specified benefits but business-as-usual has only vague benefits.

b   projects drive change whereas business-as-usual continues existing activities.

c   projects have tightly controlled budgets whereas business-as-usual does not.

d   projects have unclear deadlines but business-as-usual has multiple milestones.

Question 13

The purpose of project progress reporting is to:

a   ensure a simpler critical path.

b   enable the tracking of project deliverables.

c   ensure stakeholder acceptance of project deliverables.

d   provide an increased total float.

Question 14

Which of the following is the purpose of an estimating funnel?

a   Keeping resource usage to a minimum to help reduce costs.

b   Supporting the production of comparative estimates.

c   Identifying where costs can be minimised when preparing a budget.

d   Representing increasing levels of estimating accuracy achieved through the life cycle.

Question 15

One advantage of virtual communications is:

a   non-verbal signals can have an impact on discussions.

b   it's easy to detect signs of conflict within the project team.

c   access to a wider resource pool for the project.

d   the project team will always be co-located.

Question 16

Which technique could be used by a project manager when resources are limited?

a Resource aggregation.
b Resource estimation.
c Resource levelling.
d Resource expansion.

Question 17

The main aim of quality management is to:

a prepare a high-quality management plan.
b ensure that deliverables meet appropriate standards.
c validate the use of consistent standards.
d determine whether to accept change requests.

Question 18

Which of the following is a purpose of issue management?

a To stop issues occurring within the project.
b To address and resolve the issues that occur.
c To address and resolve uncertainty.
d To reschedule activities to reduce costs.

Question 19

Product breakdown structures illustrate the required scope of work by a hierarchical structure itemising the:

a components of each product.
b budget of each product.
c benefits of each product.
d risks of each product.

Question 20

The definition of benefits management includes which key activities?

a Planning, analysis and integration of project benefits.
b Justification, validation and acceptance of project benefits.
c Identification, tracking and realisation of project benefits.
d Realisation, acceptance and integration of project benefits.

Question 21

Which of the following statements about scheduling is false?

a Defines the sequence of activities.
b Considers work calendars and time contingency.
c Provides a baseline for safety considerations.
d Quantifies the required resources.

Question 22

Which of the following defines the term 'deployment baseline'?

a The starting point for creating a resource histogram.

b The basis for creating an organisational breakdown structure.

c The starting point for the monitoring of project risks.

d The basis for progress monitoring.

Question 23

Which of the following is an activity in a typical configuration management process?

a Evaluation.

b Identification.

c Registration.

d Justification.

Question 24

Stakeholder analysis supports effective stakeholder engagement by:

a identifying stakeholders with high levels of power and interest.

b ensuring stakeholder acceptance of project deliverables.

c justifying the preferred project option to stakeholders.

d providing information to all stakeholders.

Question 25

Which of the following is a project?

a Introducing a new information technology system.

b Operating a national rail network.

c Organising ongoing catering in the armed forces.

d Managing day-to-day security for senior politicians.

Question 26

One purpose of a typical project business case is to:

a carry out earned value analysis.

b allocate resources to the project.

c analyse cost-benefit of the project.

d plan project work packages.

Question 27

One disadvantage of physical communication is:

a its significant environmental impact when compared with other forms of communication.

b no audit trail is available for review at a later date by project team members.

c it is reliant on technology being available to all relevant members of the project.

d your body language may not reflect what you're saying when passing on information.

Question 28

One of the benefits of developing communication plans in projects is that this ensures:

a the power and influence of stakeholders is understood.

b all communication is delivered face-to-face.

c your message is understood.

d clear reporting lines for the project.

Question 29

A project life cycle which combines approaches from the linear and iterative life cycles is known as … project life cycle.

a a hybrid.

b an extended.

c a reduced.

d a combined.

Question 30

The purpose of project management is to:

a organise management plans.

b keep all stakeholders happy.

c control change initiatives.

d effect beneficial change.

Question 31

Which of the following statements refers to how scope is managed in a linear project but not an iterative project?

a Teams can act on new knowledge to change the scope.

b Teams can re-prioritise requirements within the scope.

c The scope of work is the starting point for the implementation of change control.

d Scope definition is assumed to be fixed for the whole project.

Question 32

One difference between an issue and a risk is an issue:

a must be recorded but a risk does not have to be.

b is an uncertain event but a risk is not.

c is a certain event but a risk is not.

d always affects scope but a risk does not.

Question 33

Communication includes:

1 exchanging information.
2 managing stakeholders.
3 confirming there is a shared understanding.
4 building relationships within your team.

a 2 and 3 only
b 1 and 4 only
c 1 and 3 only
d 2 and 4 only

Question 34

A project manager requires a team member to focus on the team's objectives and draw out other team members. Which of Belbin's team roles is most appropriate?

a Shaper.
b Monitor Evaluator.
c Specialist.
d Coordinator.

Question 35

An extended project life cycle can be defined as:

a an approach that adds operational and termination phases to a linear life cycle.
b an approach that adds adoption and benefits realisation phases to a linear life cycle.
c a framework for conducting a cost-benefit analysis once a project has closed.
d a framework for ensuring the redeployment of assets post-project.

Question 36

One aspect of quality planning is to:

a plan the audit of a project to provide assurance to the project board.
b provide confidence that a project will achieve its objectives in the required time frame.
c specify the acceptance criteria used to validate the outputs are fit for purpose.
d confirm routes for reporting to ensure effective communication.

Question 37

Which of the following is **not** a key element of project scope management?

a Define outputs.
b Identify outputs.
c Share outputs.
d Control outputs.

Question 38

Which of the following is a difference between deployment baselines in linear life cycles and iterative life cycles?

a Linear project life cycles set the deployment baseline for the whole project.

b In an iterative project life cycle the scope and quality are fixed in the deployment baseline.

c Only deployment baselines in iterative life cycles have an integrated baseline review.

d Only deployment baselines in linear life cycles have an integrated baseline review.

Question 39

Which of the following defines the term 'risk'?

a The potential of a situation or event to impact on the achievement of specific objectives.

b A problem that is now breaching, or is about to breach, delegated tolerances for work on a project or programme.

c Scope creep within an uncontrolled project.

d The use of estimation to determine costs, resources and activities.

Question 40

Suppliers are stakeholders of a project management plan because they:

a contribute to the project's procurement strategy.

b help satisfy the project's resource requirements.

c provide acceptance certificates based on quality of resources supplied.

d determine the quality requirements of goods supplied.

Question 41

Which of the following defines the term 'issue'?

a. A problem which is now breaching, or is about to breach, delegated tolerances for work on a project or programme.

b. A problem which occurs on a day-to-day basis and could have an immediate impact on a project.

c. A problem which has the potential to impact on the achievement of specific project objectives.

d. A problem which can only be resolved by a project manager and within the project team.

Question 42

Which of the following define leadership?

1 Ability to establish vision and direction.
2 Developing team skills that enhance project performance.
3 Empowering and inspiring people to achieve success.
4 Ability to influence and align others towards a common purpose.

a 1, 2 and 4.
b 1, 2 and 3.
c 2, 3 and 4.
d 1, 3 and 4.

Question 43

Which of the following are typical estimating methods?

1 Analytical.
2 Budgeting.
3 Analogous.
4 Parametric.

a 1, 2 and 4.
b 1, 2 and 3.
c 1, 3 and 4.
d 2, 3 and 4.

Question 44

Procurement strategy can be defined as the high-level approach for securing:

a stakeholder engagement.
b funding for the project.
c buy-in from the project sponsor.
d goods and services required for the project.

Question 45

Which of the following is **not** an output of a critical path analysis?

a Total and free float.
b Earliest start time and latest finish time of activities.
c Project completion time.
d Cost-benefit analysis.

Question 46

A project manager would use a cost breakdown structure to produce:

a the cost of a do-nothing option.
b an analytical estimate.
c high-level project costs.
d a comparative estimate.

Question 47

Which of the following is the correct sequence for the stages of a linear project life cycle?

a Deployment, Concept, Definition, Transition.
b Concept, Transition, Definition, Deployment.
c Concept, Definition, Deployment, Transition.
d Transition, Definition, Deployment, Concept.

Question 48

In the Tuckman team development model, which is the stage where team members are clear and comfortable with their roles and responsibilities, and the project manager starts to see signs of the team working together?

a Storming.
b Forming.
c Norming.
d Performing.

Question 49

Which of the following is a definition of project management?

a A complex process of supervising and managing the delivery of any time-bound deliverable.
b Any change in management techniques in a company that achieves strategic objectives.
c The application of processes, methods, knowledge, skills and experience to achieve specific objectives for change.
d The coordination of several projects alongside business-as-usual.

Question 50

Which of the following defines quality?

a The fitness for purpose of outputs and processes.
b The value for money of a product.
c The satisfaction of the stakeholders.
d The thoroughness of the management plan.

Question 51

Quality control verifies that:

a the project follows appropriate processes.
b project outputs are delivered on time.
c the project follows appropriate governance.
d project outputs meet acceptance criteria.

Question 52

The purpose of a decision gate is to decide whether:

a the response to a risk is valid.

b the project is viable in line with the business case.

c the project delivered against the success criteria.

d lessons were effectively learned during the project.

Question 53

Establishing success criteria is important at the start of the project, as they:

a indicate how the stakeholder needs will be met.

b ensure adequate resource allocation.

c indicate what is important in supplier selection.

d ensure comprehensive risk analysis.

Question 54

One purpose of risk management is to:

a adapt the plan to resolve problems.

b minimise threats and maximise opportunities.

c continually improve the project teams' efficiency.

d manage variations in a controlled way.

Question 55

Which of the following is an activity in a typical risk management process?

a Verification.

b Request.

c Closure.

d Justification.

Question 56

When an item goes through change control, which of the following must happen as part of a robust configuration management process?

a Costs associated with the change are evaluated and documented.

b Risks associated with the change are monitored to avoid delays to the project.

c The item is approved or declined in line with stakeholder expectations.

d Documents are updated to include any approved changes.

Question 57

The purpose of a risk register is to provide a:

a structured process for risk identification.

b record of the ownership of risk and issue management actions.

c means of assessing the likelihood and impact of all of the risks.

d record of risks, their impact and the actions taken to manage them.

Question 58

Which of the following is a part of change control?

a Requests for change are realised.

b Requests for change are mitigated.

c Requests for change are evaluated.

d Requests for change are resolved.

Question 59

The primary purpose of a milestone in a project is to show:

a significant events.

b resource constraints.

c task dependencies.

d critical-path highlights.

Question 60

Which of the following can be adjusted during a timebox?

1 Scope.

2 Resource.

3 Time.

4 Quality.

a 1 and 2 only.

b 1 and 4 only.

c 3 and 4 only.

d 2 and 4 only.

End of questions

Sample paper answer key

1 A	2 B	3 A	4 A	5 B	6 D
7 C	8 B	9 D	10 A	11 A	12 B
13 B	14 D	15 C	16 C	17 B	18 B
19 A	20 C	21 C	22 D	23 B	24 A
25 A	26 C	27 A	28 C	29 A	30 D
31 D	32 C	33 C	34 D	35 B	36 C
37 C	38 A	39 A	40 B	41 A	42 D
43 C	44 D	45 D	46 B	47 C	48 C
49 C	50 A	51 D	52 B	53 A	54 B
55 C	56 D	57 D	58 C	59 A	60 B

Glossary

This glossary is made up of terms that you will find in this study guide and is consistent with definitions outlined in the seventh edition of the *APM Body of Knowledge*.

Acceptance criteria The requirements and essential conditions that have to be achieved before a deliverable is accepted.

Activity (1) A task, job, operation or process consuming time and possibly other resources. (2) The smallest self-contained unit of work in a project.

Adoption The optional additional phase in a linear life cycle that facilitates the use of project outputs to enable the acceptance and use of benefits.

Agile A family of development methodologies where requirements and solutions are developed iteratively and incrementally throughout the life cycle.

Analogous estimating An estimating technique based on the comparison with, and factoring from, the cost of similar, previous work. Also known as comparative estimating.

Analytical estimating An estimating technique that uses detailed specifications to estimate time and cost for each product or activity. Also known as bottom-up estimating.

Assurance The process of providing confidence to stakeholders that projects, programmes and portfolios will achieve their objectives for beneficial change.

Baseline The reference levels against which a project, programme or portfolio is monitored and controlled.

Benefit A positive and measurable impact of change.

Benefits management The identification, definition, planning, tracking and realisation of benefits.

Benefits realisation The practice of ensuring that benefits are derived from outputs and outcomes.

Bottom-up estimating An estimating technique that uses detailed specifications to estimate time and cost for each product or activity. Also known as analytical estimating.

Breakdown structure A hierarchical structure by which project elements are decomposed. Examples include cost breakdown structure (CBS), organisational breakdown structure (OBS), product breakdown structure (PBS) and work breakdown structure (WBS).

Business-as-usual An organisation's normal day-to-day operations. Also referred to as steady-state.

Business case Provides justification for undertaking a project, programme or portfolio. It evaluates the benefit, cost and risk of alternative options and provides a rationale for the preferred solution.

Change control The process through which all requests to change the approved baseline of a project, programme or portfolio are captured, evaluated and then approved, rejected or deferred.

Change freeze A point after which no further changes to scope will be considered.

Change management The overarching approach taken in an organisation to move from the current to a future desirable state using a coordinated and structured approach in collaboration with stakeholders.

Change register (or log) A record of all proposed changes to scope.

Change request A request to obtain formal approval for changes to the approved baseline.

Closure The formal end point of a project, programme or portfolio, either because planned work has been completed or because it has been terminated early.

Communication The process of exchanging information and confirming there is shared understanding.

Comparative estimating An estimating technique based on the comparison with, and factoring from, the cost of similar, previous work. Also known as analogous estimating.

Complexity Relates to the degree of interaction of all the elements that make up a project, programme or portfolio and is dependent on such factors as the level of uncertainty, interaction between stakeholders and degree of innovation.

Concept The first phase in a linear life cycle that develops an initial idea through initial studies and high-level requirements management, and assessment of viability including an outline business case.

Configuration The functional and physical characteristics of a product as defined in its specification and achieved through the deployment of project management plans.

Configuration management Encompasses the technical and administrative activities concerned with the creation, maintenance, controlled change and quality control of the scope of work.

Conflict resolution The process of identifying and addressing differences that, if left unmanaged, would affect successful completion of objectives.

Context A collective term for the societal and/or organisational setting of a project, programme or portfolio. Also known as environment.

Contingency Provision of additional time or money to deal with the occurrence of risks should they occur. See also risk budget and management reserve.

Contract An agreement made between two or more parties that creates legally binding obligations between them. The contract sets out those obligations and the actions that can be taken if they are not met.

Control Tracking performance against agreed plans and taking the corrective action required to meet defined objectives.

Critical path A sequence of activities through a precedence network from start to finish, the sum of whose durations determines the overall duration.

Critical path analysis An activity-based scheduling technique that determines the overall duration of the identified work based on estimates and logical dependencies. The method of determining the critical path.

Decision gate A point in the life cycle between phases that is used to review and confirm the viability of the work in line with the business case. Alternatively called stage gates or gates.

Deliverable A tangible or intangible component of a project's output. Used interchangeably with product and output.

Deployment baseline The reference levels created as an output of integrated planning and the development of the project management plan.

Environment A collective term for the societal and/or organisational setting of a project, programme or portfolio. Also known as context.

Escalation The process by which issues are drawn to the attention of a higher level of management.

Estimate A forecast of the probable time or cost of completing work.

Estimating The use of a range of tools and techniques to produce forecasts of the probable time or cost of completing work.

Event-driven Control actions or reports that are triggered by a specific event.

Extended life cycle A life cycle approach that adds an adoption phase to a linear or iterative life cycle with the purpose of ensuring that the accountability and governance of the investment stays with the change teams until change is fully embedded. It provides the missing connection to benefits realisation in a linear life cycle and facilitates cooperation and knowledge-sharing between change and business-as-usual teams.

Facilitation An approach to working with groups in a collaborative way to create energy and make it easy for the group to solve problems.

Float A term used to describe the flexibility with which an activity may be rescheduled. There are various types of float, such as total float and free float.

Forecast A prediction of a defined future state, typically related to the duration and out-turn cost of a project or programme.

Funding The means by which the money required to undertake a project, programme or portfolio is secured and then made available as required.

Gantt chart A graphical representation of activity against time.

Governance The framework of authority and accountability that defines and controls the outputs, outcomes and benefits from projects, programmes and portfolios. The mechanism whereby the investing organisation exerts financial and technical control over the deployment of the work and the realisation of value.

Governance board A body that provides sponsorship to a project, programme or portfolio. The board will represent financial, provider and user interests. Members of a governance board oversee deployment and make decisions through the chosen life cycle. Alternatively called steering committee, steering group, project board, programme board, etc.

Handover The point, as part of the transition phase of a linear life cycle, where deliverables are commissioned and handed over to the permanent organisation to adopt.

Host organisation The organisation that provides the strategic direction of the project, programme or portfolio and is the primary investor and recipient of benefits. Used interchangeably with investing organisation and client organisation.

Hybrid life cycle A pragmatic approach to achieving beneficial change that combines a linear life cycle for some phases or activities with an iterative life cycle for others.

Influencing The act of affecting the behaviours and actions of others.

Information management The collection, storage, curation, dissemination, archiving and destruction of documents, images, drawings and other sources of information.

Integrated planning The application of management processes that bring together the planning of benefits, success criteria, scope, quality, time, resources, cost, risk, communications, etc. to create the project management plan.

Issue A problem that is now breaching, or is about to breach, delegated tolerances for work on a project or programme. Issues require support from the sponsor to agree a resolution.

Iterative life cycle A life cycle that repeats one or more of the phases of a project or programme before proceeding to the next one, with the objective of managing uncertainty of scope by allowing objectives to evolve as learning and discovery takes place.

Leadership The ability to establish vision and direction, to influence and align others towards a common purpose, and to empower and inspire people to achieve success.

Life cycle A framework comprising a set of distinct high-level stages required to transform an idea or concept into reality in an orderly and efficient manner. Life cycles offer a systematic and organised way to undertake project-based work and can be viewed as the structure underpinning deployment.

Linear life cycle A life cycle that aims to complete a project within a single pass through a set of distinct phases that are completed serially and span from the development of the initial concept to the deployment of an ultimate output, outcome or benefits.

Management plan A plan that sets out how an aspect of a project, programme or portfolio will be delivered, for example, a configuration management plan. Individual management plans are component parts of the overall project management plan (PMP) that is the output of integrated planning.

Management reserve A sum of money that is part of overall cost contingency to cover the cost impact of unidentified risks, and potentially some already-identified very low-probability, very high-impact risks. See also risk budget and contingency.

Milestone A key event selected for its importance in the schedule, commonly associated with tangible acceptance of deliverables.

Network diagram A model of activities and their dependencies used in scheduling. Also known as a precedence network.

Objectives A generic term for predetermined results towards which effort is directed. Objectives may be defined in terms of outputs, outcomes and/or benefits.

Opportunity A positive risk event that, if it occurs, will have an upside/beneficial effect on the achievement of one or more objectives.

Organisational culture the unwritten rules that influence individual and group behaviour and attitudes. Applicable at multiple levels of organisation, including national culture or project culture.

Outcome The changed circumstances or behaviour that results from the use of an output and leads to realisation of benefits.

Output The tangible or intangible product typically delivered by a project. Used interchangeably with deliverable and product.

Parametric estimating An estimating technique that uses a statistical relationship between historical data and other variables to calculate an estimate.

Phase The major subdivision of a life cycle.

Portfolio A collection of projects and/or programmes used to structure and manage investments at an organisational or functional level to optimise strategic benefits or operational efficiency.

Portfolio management The selection, prioritisation and control of an organisation's projects and programmes in line with its strategic objectives and capacity to deliver.

Precedence network A model of activities and their dependencies used in scheduling. Also known as a network diagram.

Procurement strategy The high-level approach for securing the goods and services required from external suppliers to satisfy project, programme and portfolio needs.

Product A tangible or intangible component of a project's output. Used interchangeably with deliverable and output.

Product owner The owner of a product who may contribute to decisions concerning the development of a product.

Programme A unique, transient strategic endeavour undertaken to achieve beneficial change and incorporating a group of related projects and business-as-usual (steady-state) activities.

Programme management The coordinated management of projects and business-as-usual (steady-state) activities to achieve beneficial change.

Project A unique, transient endeavour undertaken to bring about change and to achieve planned objectives.

Project-based working A collective term for project, programme and portfolio management. Used interchangeably with management of projects.

Project management The application of processes, methods, knowledge, skills and experience to achieve specific objectives for change.

Project (programme or portfolio) management office (PMO) An organisational structure that provides support for projects, programmes and/or portfolios.

Project management plan (PMP) The output of the process of integrated planning for a project or programme.

Project professional The term used to describe those people in roles associated with the management of projects, programmes or portfolios.

Quality The fitness for purpose or the degree of conformance of the outputs of a process, or the process itself, to requirements.

Quality control Consists of inspection, measurement and testing to verify that the project outputs meet acceptance criteria defined during quality planning.

Quality planning Takes the defined scope and specifies the acceptance criteria used to validate that the outputs are fit for purpose to the sponsor.

Report (1) The presentation of information in an appropriate format (e.g. management report). (2) A written record or summary, a detailed account or statement, or a verbal account. (3) A term used to refer to a role that is subordinate to another role in an organisation structure.

Requirements The stakeholders' wants and needs clearly defined with acceptance criteria.

Resource allocation The process by which labour and non-labour resources are attributed to activities.

Resource levelling An approach used during resource optimisation that delays activities such that resource usage is kept below specified limits. Also known as resource-limited scheduling.

Resource management The acquisition and deployment of the internal and external resources required to deliver the project, programme or portfolio.

Resource optimisation A collective term used to describe the methods for ensuring that labour and non-labour resources are matched to the schedule. See also resource levelling and resource smoothing.

Resource smoothing An approach used as part of resource optimisation that involves utilising float, or increasing or decreasing the resources required for specific activities, such that any peaks and troughs of resource usage are smoothed out, avoiding extension of the duration where possible. Also known as time-limited resource scheduling.

Resources All the labour and non-labour items required to undertake the scope of work to the required quality.

Responsibility assignment matrix A diagram or chart showing assigned responsibilities for elements of work. It is created by combining the work breakdown structure with the organisational breakdown structure.

Risk The potential of a situation or event to impact on the achievement of specific objectives.

Risk analysis An assessment and synthesis of estimating uncertainty and/or specific risk events to gain an understanding of their individual significance and/or their combined impact on objectives.

Risk analysis and management A process that allows individual risk events and overall risk to be understood and managed proactively, optimising success by minimising threats and maximising opportunities.

Risk appetite How much risk investors are willing to tolerate in achieving their objectives. Expressed as risk thresholds or tolerances.

Risk event An uncertain event or set of circumstances that would, if it occurred, have an effect on the achievement of one or more objectives.

Risk owner The individual or group best placed to assess and manage a risk.

Risk register A document listing identified risk events and their corresponding planned responses. Used interchangeably with risk log or risk repository.

Risk response An action or set of actions to reduce the probability or impact of a threat, or to increase the probability or impact of an opportunity.

Schedule A timetable showing the forecast start and finish dates for activities or events within a project, programme or portfolio.

Scope The totality of the outputs, outcomes and benefits and the work required to produce them.

Scope management The process whereby outputs, outcomes and benefits are identified, defined and controlled.

Sponsor A critical role as part of the governance board of any project, programme or portfolio. The sponsor is accountable for ensuring that the work is governed effectively and delivers the objectives that meet identified needs.

Stakeholder Individuals or groups who have an interest or role in the project, programme or portfolio, or are impacted by it.

Stakeholder engagement The systematic identification, analysis, planning and implementation of actions designed to influence stakeholders.

Statement of work An annex to the main body of a contract that defines the detail of deliverables, timescales and management procedures relevant to the contract.

Strategic intent The term used to describe the aspirational plans, overarching purpose or intended direction of travel needed to reach an organisational vision.

Success criteria The satisfaction of stakeholder needs for the deployment of a project. Note this is a different performance measure to benefits, which are focused on the strategic intent and delivering beneficial change.

Sustainability An approach to business that balances the environmental, social, economic and administrative aspects of project-based working to meet the current needs of stakeholders without compromising or overburdening future generations.

Team A group of people working in collaboration or by cooperation towards a common goal.

Temporary organisation (team) A generic term used to describe a specific project, programme or portfolio team brought together specifically to implement project-based work. Used to contrast the organisational structure for project-based work from the permanent organisation.

Threat A negative risk event; a risk event that, if it occurs, will have a downside/detrimental effect on one or more objectives.

Timebox A generic term used in iterative life cycle approaches to refer to an iteration with a fixed end date that is not allowed to change, thereby adjusting the scope and quality to deliver on time and to cost.

Tolerance A level of delegated permission to vary performance from specified parameters.

Transition The fourth phase in a linear cycle, where results are handed over, commissioned and accepted by the sponsor, culminating in formal closure.

Triple constraint A way of describing the fundamental trade-off between time, cost and quality in delivering the scope of a project. Often also called the iron triangle.

Users The group of people who are intended to work with deliverables to enable beneficial change to be realised.

Value A standard, principle or quality considered worthwhile or desirable. In value management terms, value is defined as the ratio of 'satisfaction of requirements' over 'use of resources'.

Virtual team A team where the people are separated by geography and potentially time zone.

References

Figure 2.1.5.2 *DSDM Agile Project Framework Handbook,* 2014. Reproduced with the kind permission of the Agile Business Consortium. https://www.agilebusiness.org

Figure 2.3.4.3 Belbin Associates for the Belbin 'Team Roles', as defined by Dr Meredith Belbin. Reproduced by kind permission of www.belbin.com

Index

S

schedule management 45

schedule status 78

schedules 91

scheduling 134
  purpose 69
  resource scheduling and optimisation 69–76, 119–122

scope definition 113

scope management 56–64, 113–116, 137
  definition 56
  in iterative life cycles 114
  within linear and iterative projects 57

scope verification 58

self-assessment
  examination practice 129–142
  test questions and answers 87–128

'send to all' syndrome 123

service-level agreements 76

SMP see sustainability management plan (SMP)

sociological factors 9

sponsors 19, 24, 94
  decision gates 54
  managing expectations of 95
  responsibilities of 19, 94, 132

stakeholder analysis 37–39, 102, 103, 135

stakeholder engagement 37–39, 102–104

stakeholder management 103

stakeholders 9, 37, 77, 102
  approving and rejecting changes 116
  communication with 41–42
  governance board 94
  power–interest matrix 38
  project management plan 33–35, 138

stand-alone projects 76

statement of work 36, 148

status accounting 60, 63

steering group 11, 19, 24, 78

strategic direction 94

strategy 7, 12
  engagement 39, 41
  management 34
  procurement 76

study groups 4, 6

study guide planner 3

subject matter experts 25

success 65
  planning for 36–64

success criteria 35, 102, 141

success factors 52, 61

suppliers 25, 39, 76, 121, 138

supply chain 76

sustainability 11, 148

sustainability management plan (SMP) 11

T

team development 82
  adjourning stage 83
  forming stage 83, 125
  norming stage 83
  performing stage 83, 125
  storming stage 83

team leaders see project managers

team members 20, 78, 81

team performance 80

team roles
  action roles 85
  personality orientation and 125
  social roles 85
  thinking roles 85

teams 65, 82
  building and maintaining 124
  challenges when developing and leading 81–82
  dispersed 86
  effective 124
  models to assist team development 82–85, 125

teamwork 80

technological factors 9

test questions 87–125

threats 8, 45, 108

time 120

time constraint 13

time-limited scheduling see resource smoothing

timeboxing 73, 99, 142

timeline 34

total float 71, 74, 119

Tuckman team development model 82–83, 140

U

V

W